THE
DELICIOUSLY
CHEESY
COOKBOOK

13-Digit ISBN: 978-1-64643-188-5
10-Digit ISBN: 1-64643-188-X

This book may be ordered by mail from the publisher. Please include $5.99 for postage and handling. Please support your local bookseller first!

Books published by Cider Mill Press Book Publishers are available at special discounts for bulk purchases in the United States by corporations, institutions, and other organizations. For more information, please contact the publisher.

Cider Mill Press Book Publishers
"Where Good Books Are Ready for Press"
501 Nelson Place
Nashville, Tennessee 37214

cidermillpress.com

Typography: Kepler, Acumin Pro

Image Credits: Pages 11, 14–15, 20, 23, 31, 40–41, 63, 72, 83, 84, 90–91, 92, 96, 99, 114–115, 116, 119, 120, 123, 124, 126, 131, 134, 145, 146, 149, 169, 170, 173, 174, 177, 195, 211, 220, 223, and 228 courtesy of Cider Mill Press. All other images used under official license from Shutterstock.com.

Front Cover Image: Potato Gratin, see page 17
Front End Page: French Onion Soup, see page 127
Back End Page: Cream Cheese Frosting, see page 193

Printed in Malaysia

23 24 25 26 27 TJM 6 5 4 3 2

THE DELICIOUSLY CHEESY COOKBOOK

OVER 100 CHEESY COMFORT FOODS FOR EVERY CRAVING

CIDER MILL PRESS

BOOK PUBLISHERS

CONTENTS

INTRODUCTION

So often, the things that transform our world and our lives have little to do with our grand plans, our brilliance, our will. Instead, they are come upon by happenstance, via indolence or accident.

Penicillin was able to revolutionize the medical world only because Alexander Fleming wasn't terribly fastidious about clean lab equipment. The paradigm-shifting discovery of the Big Bang was stumbled into following a concerted effort to clean pigeon droppings out of a radio antenna. The vulcanized rubber that, when transformed into tires, makes it possible for billions of people and most of the food we consume to travel safely over the world's roads, came about due to the clumsiness of Charles Goodyear, who fortuitously dropped one of his many rubbery concoctions on a hot stove.

At the apex of the happy accidents that have left an indelible mark upon mankind resides cheese. Because one person left a bit of milk sitting for too long, the rest of us have been granted endless enjoyment.

An unfortunate few may see not see this cheesy present from chance as sitting comfortably above the other achievements mentioned. But most of you are nodding along knowingly, having long believed that our unlikely hero's daring decision to taste the curds that had formed in the milk produced something truly transcendent.

This book is a celebration of all that has resulted from that one grand act, a showcase for all of the deliciousness cheese is capable of. Whether you're interested in adding complexity, depth, and silkiness to a soup, comforting your inner child, bringing a simple salad to life, or composing an exceptional board for you and your friends to gossip over, you'll soon see that all you have to do is say cheese.

APPETIZERS, SNACKS & SIDES

A large part of cheese's innate culinary genius is its ability to facilitate a simple approach. By doing nothing more than flanking it with a few fresh vegetables, stuffing it into a flaky wrapper, or folding it into a bread dough, you can bolster a preparation's taste and texture, add complexity, and guarantee an enjoyable experience.

This talent is most noticeable in the preparations gathered in this chapter, providing the cheese lover dozens of quick and easy dishes that guarantee their one true love crosses their path each and every day.

CAPRESE SALAD

YIELD: **4 SERVINGS** | ACTIVE TIME: **5 MINUTES** | TOTAL TIME: **5 MINUTES**

INGREDIENTS

1 lb. in-season heirloom tomatoes, sliced

Salt and pepper, to taste

1 lb. fresh mozzarella cheese, sliced

¼ cup Pesto (see page 66)

Quality extra-virgin olive oil, to taste

1 Season the tomatoes with salt and pepper. While alternating, arrange them and the slices of mozzarella on a platter.

2 Drizzle the Pesto and olive oil over the tomatoes and mozzarella and enjoy.

GOAT CHEESE, OLIVE & FENNEL PHYLLO TRIANGLES

YIELD: **16 SERVINGS** | ACTIVE TIME: **30 MINUTES** | TOTAL TIME: **1 HOUR AND 30 MINUTES**

INGREDIENTS

1 tablespoon extra-virgin olive oil

½ fennel bulb, trimmed, cored, and chopped

2 garlic cloves, minced

6 tablespoons white wine

1 tablespoon Pernod

1 tablespoon minced raisins

6 green olives, pits removed, minced

1 cup crumbled goat cheese

1 tablespoon finely chopped fresh chives

1 teaspoon lemon zest

1 teaspoon fresh lemon juice

Salt and pepper, to taste

½ lb. frozen phyllo dough, thawed

6 tablespoons unsalted butter, melted

1 tablespoon black sesame seeds

1 Place the olive oil in a medium saucepan and warm it over medium heat. Add the fennel and cook, stirring occasionally, until it has softened and is starting to brown, about 8 minutes.

2 Add the garlic and cook, stirring continually, until fragrant, about 1 minute. Add the white wine, Pernod, and raisins and cook until the liquid has evaporated, about 5 minutes. Remove the pan from heat and let the mixture cool for 5 minutes.

3 Place the olives, goat cheese, chives, lemon zest, and lemon juice in a mixing bowl and stir to combine. Add the fennel mixture, fold to combine, and season the mixture with salt and pepper. Set the filling aside.

4 Preheat the oven to 425°F. Line a baking sheet with parchment paper. Place a piece of parchment paper on a work surface. Lay one sheet of phyllo on the parchment and brush it with some of the butter. Lay another sheet of phyllo on top and gently press down. Brush the phyllo with butter and then cut the rectangle into 2-inch-wide strips. Make sure to cover the rest of the phyllo dough so that it does not dry out.

5 Place 2 teaspoons of the filling at the bottom of each strip and shape the filling into a triangle. Taking care to maintain that triangle shape, roll up the strip, as if you were folding a flag. Crimp the folded-up pastries to seal them and place them, seam side down, on the baking sheet.

6 Repeat Steps 4 and 5 until you have 16 filled pastries.

7 Sprinkle the sesame seeds over the pastries, place them in the oven, and bake until golden brown, about 10 minutes.

8 Remove from the oven and let the pastries cool before serving.

STUFFED AVOCADOS

YIELD: **2 SERVINGS** | ACTIVE TIME: **45 MINUTES** | TOTAL TIME: **1 HOUR AND 30 MINUTES**

INGREDIENTS

1 cup finely diced butternut squash

2 tablespoons extra-virgin olive oil

1 teaspoon kosher salt

1 teaspoon black pepper

2 ripe avocados

½ cup crumbled feta cheese

2 tablespoons Aioli (see page 235)

1   Preheat the oven to 450°F. In a bowl, combine the squash with 1 tablespoon of the olive oil, the salt, and pepper. Transfer the squash to a baking sheet, place it in the oven, and roast until lightly browned and soft enough to mash, 15 to 20 minutes. Remove the squash from the oven and set it aside.

2   Halve the avocados and remove their seeds. Using a spoon, remove the avocado flesh and place it in a bowl. Add the feta and roasted squash and mash the mixture until it is smooth and well combined.

3   Fill the avocado skins with the mixture and lightly brush the top of each one with the remaining oil. Place them on a baking sheet and place them in the oven.

4   Roast until the tops of the avocados are browned, 10 to 15 minutes. Remove from the oven, drizzle the aioli over the top, and enjoy.

Stuffed Avocados, *see page 13*

POTATO GRATIN

YIELD: **4 SERVINGS** | ACTIVE TIME: **20 MINUTES** | TOTAL TIME: **45 MINUTES**

INGREDIENTS

4 tablespoons unsalted butter, cubed, plus more as needed

2 lbs. russet potatoes, peeled and sliced thin

2 garlic cloves, smashed

1 bay leaf

2 tablespoons whole milk

1 teaspoon kosher salt, plus more to taste

4 oz. cheddar cheese, grated

Freshly grated nutmeg, to taste

Black pepper, to taste

¾ cup heavy cream, plus more as needed

1   Preheat the oven to 375°F. While the oven is heating up, coat a baking dish with butter.

2   Place the potatoes in a saucepan with the garlic, bay leaf, milk, and salt. Bring the mixture to a boil over high heat, drain the potatoes, and discard the bay leaf.

3   Place half of the potatoes in the baking dish and then sprinkle half of the cheddar, a pinch of nutmeg, salt, and pepper over them. Add the cream and 2 tablespoons of the butter. Place the remaining potatoes on top and repeat with the cheddar, nutmeg, salt, pepper, and butter.

4   Place the dish in the oven and bake until the potatoes are tender and the top of the dish is browned and crispy, 25 to 30 minutes. The cream should come halfway up the potatoes at the start and cook down to a rich sauce by the end.

5   Remove the gratin from the oven and let it cool briefly before enjoying.

ASPARAGUS TART

YIELD: **8 SERVINGS** | ACTIVE TIME: **15 MINUTES** | TOTAL TIME: **45 MINUTES**

INGREDIENTS

½ teaspoon kosher salt, plus more to taste

1 lb. asparagus, trimmed

1½ cups ricotta cheese

¼ cup extra-virgin olive oil

2 tablespoons heavy cream

2 egg yolks

1 teaspoon chopped fresh rosemary

1 Savory Tart Shell (see page 236)

1 Preheat the oven to 350°F. Bring water to a boil in a large saucepan. Add salt until the water tastes just shy of seawater, add the asparagus, and cook for 2 minutes. Drain the asparagus, pat it dry, and set it aside.

2 Place all of the remaining ingredients, aside from the tart shell, in a mixing bowl and stir to combine. Distribute the mixture evenly in the tart shell, arrange the asparagus on top, and place the tart in the oven. Bake until the custard is set and golden brown, about 25 minutes.

3 Remove the tart from the oven and serve warm or at room temperature.

COUSCOUS-STUFFED TOMATOES

YIELD: **4 SERVINGS** | ACTIVE TIME: **30 MINUTES** | TOTAL TIME: **1 HOUR AND 30 MINUTES**

INGREDIENTS

4 tomatoes

2 teaspoons sugar

Salt and pepper, to taste

2 tablespoons plus 1 teaspoon extra-virgin olive oil

¼ cup panko

1 cup freshly grated Manchego cheese

1 onion, chopped

2 garlic cloves, minced

⅛ teaspoon red pepper flakes

4 cups baby spinach

¾ cup couscous

1½ cups Chicken Stock (see page 239)

2 tablespoons chopped Kalamata olives

2 teaspoons red wine vinegar

1. Preheat the oven to 350°F. Cut the top ½ inch off the tomatoes and scoop out their insides. Sprinkle the sugar and some salt into the tomatoes, turn them upside down, and place them on a wire rack. Let the tomatoes drain for 30 minutes.

2. Place 1 teaspoon of the olive oil in a large skillet and warm it over medium heat. Add the panko and cook, stirring continually, until golden brown, about 3 minutes. Remove the panko from the pan, place it in a bowl, and let it cool.

3. Stir half of the cheese into the cooled panko and set the mixture aside.

4. Place 1 tablespoon of the olive oil in a clean large skillet and warm it over medium-high heat. Add the onion and cook, stirring occasionally, until it has softened, about 5 minutes. Add the garlic and red pepper flakes and cook, stirring continually, for 1 minute.

5. Add the spinach and cook until it has wilted, about 2 minutes. Add the couscous and stock and bring the mixture to a simmer. Cover the pan, remove it from heat, and let it sit until the couscous is tender, about 7 minutes.

6. Fluff the couscous with a fork, add the olives, vinegar, and remaining cheese, and fold until incorporated. Season the stuffing with salt and pepper and set it aside.

7. Place the remaining olive oil in a baking dish. Add the tomatoes, cavities facing up, and fill them with the stuffing. Top with the toasted panko mixture and place the tomatoes in the oven. Roast until the tomatoes are tender, about 20 minutes.

8. Remove the tomatoes from the oven and let them cool slightly before enjoying.

STUFFED PRUNES

YIELD: **4 SERVINGS** | ACTIVE TIME: **10 MINUTES** | TOTAL TIME: **10 MINUTES**

INGREDIENTS

15 dried prunes

3 oz. blue cheese, crumbled

1   Cut a slit in the top of each prune, stuff them with the blue cheese, and either serve immediately or chill in the refrigerator. If refrigerating, let the stuffed prunes come to room temperature before serving.

CHEESE TWISTS

YIELD: **12 SERVINGS** | ACTIVE TIME: **15 MINUTES** | TOTAL TIME: **30 MINUTES**

INGREDIENTS

2 sheets of frozen puff pastry, thawed

All-purpose flour, as needed

½ cup freshly grated Fontina cheese

½ cup freshly grated Parmesan cheese

1 teaspoon finely chopped fresh thyme

1 teaspoon black pepper

1 egg, beaten

1   Preheat the oven to 375°F and line a baking sheet with parchment paper. Place the sheets of puff pastry on a flour-dusted surface and roll them out until the sheets are approximately 10 x 12–inch rectangles.

2   Place the cheeses, thyme, and pepper in a mixing bowl and stir to combine.

3   Lightly brush the tops of the pastry sheets with the egg. Sprinkle the cheese mixture over them and gently press down so it adheres to the pastry. Cut the sheets into ¼-inch-wide strips and twist them.

4   Place the twists on the baking sheet, place in the oven, and bake for 12 to 15 minutes, until the twists are golden brown and puffy. Turn the twists over and bake for another 2 to 3 minutes. Remove from the oven and let the twists cool on a wire rack before serving.

RUSTICO WITH HONEY GLAZE

YIELD: **8 SERVINGS** | ACTIVE TIME: **15 MINUTES** | TOTAL TIME: **30 MINUTES**

INGREDIENTS

Canola oil, as needed

4 sheets of frozen puff pastry, thawed

½ lb. fresh mozzarella cheese, cut into 8 slices

1 cup honey

1   Add canola oil to a Dutch oven until it is 2 inches deep and warm it to 350°F. Cut eight 5-inch circles and eight 4-inch circles from the sheets of puff pastry. Place a slice of cheese in the center of each 5-inch circle. Place a 4-inch circle over the cheese, fold the bottom circle over the edge, and pinch to seal.

2   Gently slip one or two rustici in the oil and fry until the dough is a light golden brown and crispy, about 2 to 3 minutes. Remove from oil and transfer to a paper towel–lined wire rack. Repeat until all eight wraps have been fried. To serve, drizzle honey over the top of each rustico.

SOUTHWESTERN SLIDERS

YIELD: **6 SERVINGS** | ACTIVE TIME: **20 MINUTES** | TOTAL TIME: **35 MINUTES**

INGREDIENTS

1 large egg

2 chipotle chile peppers in adobo

2 tablespoons whole milk

½ cup bread crumbs

½ cup grated jalapeño jack cheese

3 tablespoons finely chopped fresh cilantro

3 tablespoons canned diced green chilies, drained

4 garlic cloves, minced

1 tablespoon dried oregano

1 tablespoon smoked paprika

2 teaspoons cumin

1¼ lbs. ground beef

Salt and pepper, to taste

Slider rolls, for serving

1   Preheat a gas or charcoal grill to medium heat (450°F). Place the egg, chipotles, milk, and bread crumbs in a food processor and puree until smooth. Place the mixture in a mixing bowl, add the cheese, cilantro, green chilies, garlic, oregano, paprika, and cumin, and stir until thoroughly combined.

2   Stir in the beef and season the mixture with salt and pepper. Working with wet hands, form the mixture into 3-inch patties. Place the sliders on the grill and cook until cooked through, about 10 minutes. Remove the sliders from the grill, transfer to a platter, and tent loosely with aluminum foil.

3   Let the sliders rest for 10 minutes before serving with slider rolls and your favorite burger fixings.

MUSHROOM TOAST WITH WHIPPED GOAT CHEESE

YIELD: **4 SERVINGS** | ACTIVE TIME: **10 MINUTES** | TOTAL TIME: **45 MINUTES**

INGREDIENTS

½ lb. mushrooms, sliced

2 tablespoons extra-virgin olive oil

Salt, to taste

4 thick slices of sourdough bread

½ cup heavy cream

4 oz. goat cheese, softened

½ cup sunflower seeds

1 tablespoon chopped fresh rosemary

1 tablespoon honey

1 Preheat the oven to 400°F. Place the mushrooms on a baking sheet, drizzle half of the olive oil over them, and season with salt. Place the mushrooms in the oven and roast until they begin to darken, about 10 to 15 minutes. Place the slices of bread on another baking sheet, brush the tops with the remaining oil, and season with salt. Place the slices of bread in the oven and bake until golden brown, about 10 minutes.

2 While the mushrooms and bread are in the oven, place the cream in a mixing bowl and beat until stiff peaks begin to form. Add the goat cheese and beat until well combined.

3 Remove the mushrooms and toast from the oven and let them cool slightly. Spread the cream-and-goat-cheese mixture on the toast, top with the mushrooms, sunflower seeds, and rosemary, and drizzle with the honey.

POUTINE

YIELD: **4 TO 6 SERVINGS** | ACTIVE TIME: **35 MINUTES** | TOTAL TIME: **45 MINUTES**

INGREDIENTS

Canola oil, as needed

2 russet potatoes, cut into ¼ x ¼-inch fries

Salt and pepper, to taste

4 tablespoons unsalted butter

¼ cup all-purpose flour

1 garlic clove, minced

4 cups Beef Stock (see page 238)

2 tablespoons ketchup

1 tablespoon apple cider vinegar

1½ teaspoons Worcestershire sauce

2 cups cheese curds

1   Add canola oil to a Dutch oven until it is about 2 inches deep and warm it to 275°F. Gently slip the potatoes into the hot oil and fry for 5 minutes, stirring occasionally. Use a slotted spoon to remove the potatoes, transfer them to a paper towel–lined plate, and let them cool completely.

2   Warm the canola oil to 350°F. Return the cooled, once-fried potatoes to the hot oil and fry until crispy and golden brown, about 5 minutes, stirring occasionally. Transfer the French fries to a paper towel–lined plate and season them with salt.

3   Place the butter in a medium saucepan and melt it over medium-high heat. Add the flour and cook, stirring continually, until the mixture is smooth, about 2 minutes.

4   Add the garlic and cook until it has softened, about 2 minutes. Stir in the stock, ketchup, vinegar, and Worcestershire sauce, season the mixture with salt and pepper, and bring it to a boil. Cook, stirring frequently, until the gravy has thickened, about 6 minutes.

5   Remove the pan from heat and pour the gravy over the fries. Top with the cheese curds and enjoy immediately.

FRIED FETA

YIELD: **2 SERVINGS** | ACTIVE TIME: **25 MINUTES** | TOTAL TIME: **25 MINUTES**

INGREDIENTS

1 cup all-purpose flour

1 teaspoon kosher salt

1 teaspoon baking powder

1 cup water

Canola oil, as needed

1 block of feta cheese
(½ inch thick)

1 teaspoon extra-virgin
olive oil

1 cup grape tomatoes

Leaves from ½ head of
romaine lettuce

1 tablespoon Balsamic
Glaze (see page 241)

1 Place the flour, salt, baking powder, and water in a small bowl and whisk until the mixture is smooth.

2 Add canola oil to a small saucepan until it is about 1 inch deep and warm it over medium-high heat.

3 Carefully dip the block of feta in the batter until it is completely coated.

4 Submerge half of the feta in the canola oil for 5 seconds, then release it so that it floats. Fry for 1½ minutes on each side, while keeping a close eye on the feta; if the batter doesn't seal, the feta will ooze out, and this won't work. Once the feta has browned, remove from the oil and set it on a cooling rack.

5 Place the olive oil in a medium skillet and warm it over high heat. Add the tomatoes and cook until they start to blister, 2 to 3 minutes. Add the lettuce leaves and brown them for about 1 minute. Remove the pan from heat.

6 To serve, place the lettuce in a shallow bowl, scatter the tomatoes on top, and nestle the fried block of feta on top. Drizzle the Balsamic Glaze over the cheese and enjoy.

HAM & CHEESE CROISSANTS

YIELD: **16 CROISSANTS** | ACTIVE TIME: **30 MINUTES** | TOTAL TIME: **2 HOURS**

INGREDIENTS

1 sheet of frozen puff
pastry, thawed

⅔ cup Dijon mustard

16 slices of smoked ham

16 slices of Swiss cheese

1 egg, beaten

1   Preheat the oven to 400°F and line two baking sheets with parchment paper. Roll out the sheet of puff pastry until it is very thin. Using a pizza cutter or a chef's knife, cut the puff pastry into rectangles, and then cut each rectangle diagonally, yielding 16 triangles. Gently roll out each triangle until it is 8 inches long.

2   Spread 2 teaspoons of the mustard toward the wide side of each triangle. Lay a slice of the ham over the mustard and top it with a slice of the cheese, making sure to leave 1 inch of dough uncovered at the tip of each croissant.

3   Roll the croissants up tight, moving from the wide side of the triangle to the tip. Tuck the tips under the croissants. Place 8 croissants on each of the baking sheets and brush them with the beaten egg.

4   Place the croissants in the oven and bake until they are golden brown, 20 to 22 minutes. Remove the croissants from the oven and place them on wire racks. Let the croissants cool slightly before enjoying.

Ham & Cheese Croissants, see page 35

EVERYTHING CROISSANTS

YIELD: **16 CROISSANTS** | ACTIVE TIME: **30 MINUTES** | TOTAL TIME: **2 HOURS**

INGREDIENTS

1 lb. cream cheese, softened

1 sheet of frozen puff pastry, thawed

1 egg, beaten

Everything Seasoning (see page 241), for topping

1   Place the cream cheese in a piping bag. Preheat the oven to 400°F and line two baking sheets with parchment paper. Roll out the sheet of puff pastry until it is very thin. Using a pizza cutter or a chef's knife, cut the puff pastry into rectangles, and then cut each rectangle diagonally, yielding 16 triangles. Gently roll out each triangle until it is 8 inches long.

2   Cut a hole in the piping bag and pipe about 3 tablespoons of cream cheese toward the wide side of each triangle. Spread the cream cheese out a bit with an offset spatula.

3   Roll the croissants up tight, moving from the wide side of the triangle to the tip. Tuck the tips under the croissants. Place eight croissants on each of the baking sheets.

4   Brush the croissants with the egg. Sprinkle some of the seasoning over each of the croissants. Place the croissants in the oven and bake until they are golden brown, 20 to 22 minutes. Remove the croissants from the oven and place them on wire racks. Let the croissants cool slightly before enjoying.

FRIED BRUSSELS SPROUTS WITH FETA

YIELD: **4 SERVINGS** | ACTIVE TIME: **15 MINUTES** | TOTAL TIME: **15 MINUTES**

INGREDIENTS

Canola oil, as needed

3 cups small Brussels sprouts, trimmed

2 tablespoons tahini paste

1 tablespoon fresh lemon juice

½ cup crumbled feta cheese

Pinch of kosher salt

1   Add canola oil to a Dutch oven until it is about 2 inches deep and warm it to 350°F.

2   Gently slip the Brussels sprouts into the hot oil, working in batches to avoid crowding the pot. Fry the Brussels sprouts until golden brown, about 4 minutes, turning them as necessary. Remove one Brussels sprout to test that it is done—let it cool briefly and see if the inside is tender enough. Transfer the fried Brussels sprouts to a paper towel–lined plate.

3   Place the Brussels sprouts, tahini, lemon juice, and feta in a mixing bowl and stir until combined. Sprinkle the salt over the dish and enjoy.

Fried Brussels Sprouts with Feta, *see page 39*

BUFFALO WINGS WITH BLUE CHEESE DRESSING

YIELD: **4 SERVINGS** | ACTIVE TIME: **30 MINUTES** | TOTAL TIME: **45 MINUTES**

INGREDIENTS

4 tablespoons unsalted butter

1 tablespoon white vinegar

¾ cup hot sauce

1 teaspoon cayenne pepper

Canola oil, as needed

2 lbs. chicken wings

1 cup cornstarch

Salt, to taste

¼ cup sour cream

¼ cup mayonnaise

¼ cup buttermilk

1 tablespoon fresh lemon juice

Pinch of black pepper

1 cup crumbled blue cheese

Celery sticks, for serving

1 Place the butter in a large saucepan and melt it over medium heat. When it has melted, whisk in the vinegar, hot sauce, and cayenne, making sure not to breathe in the spicy steam. Remove the pan from heat and cover the sauce to keep it warm.

2 Add canola oil to a large Dutch oven until it is about 2 inches deep and gradually warm it to 375°F over medium heat.

3 Pat the chicken wings dry and dredge them in the cornstarch until completely coated. Working in batches to avoid crowding the pot, gently slip the chicken wings into the warm oil and fry until they are golden brown and crispy, about 10 minutes. Transfer the fried chicken wings to a wire rack and season them with salt.

4 Add the fried chicken wings to the spicy sauce in the saucepan and toss until they are coated. Remove them with a slotted spoon and arrange them on a platter.

5 Place the sour cream, mayonnaise, buttermilk, lemon juice, and pepper in a bowl and whisk to combine. Add the blue cheese, stir to incorporate, and serve the blue cheese dressing and celery alongside the chicken wings.

FIG, PROSCIUTTO & CAMEMBERT TART

YIELD: **6 SERVINGS** | ACTIVE TIME: **45 MINUTES** | TOTAL TIME: **1 HOUR AND 30 MINUTES**

INGREDIENTS

2 tablespoons extra-virgin olive oil

½ onion, sliced thin

½ lb. prosciutto, torn

1 Perfect Piecrust
(see page 248)

All-purpose flour,
for dusting

1 tablespoon Dijon mustard

1 round of Camembert cheese, softened

8 fresh figs, stems removed, halved

3 tablespoons balsamic vinegar

1 tablespoon honey

¼ cup arugula

1   Preheat the oven to 400°F and line a baking sheet with parchment paper. Place the olive oil in a skillet and warm it over medium heat. Add the onion and cook, stirring occasionally, until it is lightly browned, about 6 minutes. Add the prosciutto to the skillet and cook, stirring continuously, for 1 minute. Remove the skillet from heat.

2   Place the crust on a flour-dusted work surface and roll it out to 12 inches. Place it on the baking sheet, spread the Dijon mustard evenly over the crust, and top it with the onion-and-prosciutto mixture. Cut the Camembert into wedges and place them on top. Then, arrange the figs on the tart. In a small bowl, whisk the balsamic vinegar and honey together and drizzle the mixture over the tart.

3   Place the baking sheet in the oven and bake the tart until the crust is golden brown and the figs are tender, about 25 minutes.

4   Remove the tart from the oven and let it cool slightly. Top the tart with the arugula and enjoy.

MARINATED MOZZARELLA

YIELD: **4 SERVINGS** | ACTIVE TIME: **5 MINUTES** | TOTAL TIME: **5 MINUTES**

INGREDIENTS

1 (7 oz.) container
of miniature balls of
mozzarella cheese

Pesto (see page 66)

1   Place the mozzarella and Pesto in a mixing bowl, toss until the cheese is coated, and serve immediately.

FRIED SQUASH BLOSSOMS

YIELD: **4 SERVINGS** | ACTIVE TIME: **20 MINUTES** | TOTAL TIME: **50 MINUTES**

INGREDIENTS

10 squash blossoms, stamens removed

1 bunch of fresh spearmint

2 cups shredded queso fresco

Zest and juice of 1 lemon

Salt, to taste

1 cup all-purpose flour

1 teaspoon baking powder

2 egg yolks

1 cup seltzer water

2 cups canola oil

1   Place the squash blossoms on a paper towel–lined baking sheet.

2   Finely chop the spearmint and combine it with the queso fresco. Add the lemon zest and juice, season the mixture with salt, and stir to combine.

3   Stuff the squash blossoms with the mixture, taking care not to tear the flowers.

4   In a small bowl, combine the flour, baking powder, egg yolks, and seltzer water and work the mixture with a whisk until it is a smooth batter. Let the batter rest for 20 minutes.

5   Place the canola oil in a deep skillet and warm it to 350°F over medium heat.

6   Fold the tips of the squash blossoms closed and dip them into the batter. Gently slip them into the oil and fry until crispy and golden brown all over, about 2 minutes, making sure you only turn the squash blossoms once.

7   Drain the fried squash blossoms on the baking sheet. Season them lightly with salt and enjoy.

Fried Squash Blossoms, see page 47

VEGETARIAN TAQUITOS

YIELD: **4 SERVINGS** | ACTIVE TIME: **20 MINUTES** | TOTAL TIME: **35 MINUTES**

INGREDIENTS

2 poblano chile peppers

2 cups ricotta cheese

Salt, to taste

8 Corn Tortillas (see page 243)

¼ cup extra-virgin olive oil

1 Roast the poblanos over an open flame, on the grill, or in the oven until they are charred all over. Place the poblanos in a bowl, cover the bowl with plastic wrap, and let the chiles steam for 10 minutes. When cool enough to handle, remove the skins, seeds, and stems from the poblanos and dice the remaining flesh.

2 Stir the poblanos into the ricotta, season the mixture with salt, and set the mixture aside.

3 Place the tortillas in a large, dry cast-iron skillet and warm them for 30 seconds on each side. Fill the tortillas with the cheese-and-poblano mixture and roll them up tight, tucking in the ends of the tortillas so that the taquitos do not come apart.

4 Place the olive oil in the skillet and warm it over medium heat. Place the tortillas in the pan, seam side down, and cook for 1 minute before turning them over. Cook the taquitos until browned all over, about 5 minutes.

5 Transfer the taquitos to a paper towel–lined plate and let them drain before enjoying.

CRAB RANGOON

YIELD: **6 SERVINGS** | ACTIVE TIME: **25 MINUTES** | TOTAL TIME: **45 MINUTES**

INGREDIENTS

1 lb. cream cheese, softened

6 oz. fresh crabmeat

2 tablespoons confectioners' sugar

¼ teaspoon kosher salt

40 square Wonton Wrappers (see page 244)

Canola oil, as needed

1 Place the cream cheese, crabmeat, confectioners' sugar, and salt in a medium bowl and fold the mixture until it is well combined.

2 Place 1 tablespoon of the mixture in the middle of a wrapper. Rub the wrapper's edge with a moist finger, bring the corners together, and pinch to seal tightly. Transfer the dumpling to a parchment-lined baking sheet and repeat with the remaining wrappers and filling.

3 Add canola oil to a cast-iron Dutch oven until it is 2 inches deep and warm it to 325°F over medium heat. Working in batches to avoid crowding the pot, gently slip the dumplings into the hot oil and fry, while turning, until golden all over, about 3 minutes. Transfer the cooked dumplings to a paper towel–lined wire rack and let them cool briefly before enjoying.

PEA & PARMESAN DIP

YIELD: **2 CUPS** | ACTIVE TIME: **10 MINUTES** | TOTAL TIME: **20 MINUTES**

INGREDIENTS

Salt and pepper, to taste

3 cups peas

1 cup water

3 tablespoons pine nuts

1 cup freshly grated
Parmesan cheese

1 garlic clove, minced

½ cup fresh mint, chopped

1   Bring water to a boil in a large saucepan. Add salt and the peas and cook
    until the peas are bright green and warmed through, about 2 minutes.

2   Transfer half of the peas to a food processor. Add the water, pine nuts,
    Parmesan, and garlic and blitz until pureed.

3   Place the puree in a serving dish, add the peas and mint, and fold
    to incorporate. Season the dip with salt and pepper and chill in the
    refrigerator until ready to serve.

ARANCINI

YIELD: **8 SERVINGS** | ACTIVE TIME: **30 MINUTES** | TOTAL TIME: **1 HOUR AND 30 MINUTES**

INGREDIENTS

5 cups Chicken Stock
(see page 239)

½ cup unsalted butter

2 cups Arborio rice

1 small white onion, grated

1 cup white wine

4 oz. Fontina cheese,
grated, plus more
for garnish

Salt and pepper, to taste

Canola oil, as needed

6 large eggs, beaten

5 cups panko

Marinara Sauce (see page
245), for serving

1   Bring the stock to a simmer in a large saucepan. In a large skillet, melt the butter over high heat. Add the rice and onion to the skillet and cook until the rice has a toasty fragrance, about 3 minutes. Deglaze the skillet with the white wine and cook until the rice has almost completely absorbed the wine.

2   Reduce the heat to medium-high and begin adding the stock ¼ cup at a time, stirring until it has been absorbed by the rice. Continue adding the stock until the rice is al dente.

3   Turn off the heat, stir in the cheese, and season the risotto with salt and pepper. Pour it onto a rimmed baking sheet and let cool.

4   Add canola oil to a Dutch oven until it is 2 inches deep and warm it to 350°F. When the risotto is cool, form it into golf ball–sized spheres. Dredge them in the eggs and then the panko until completely coated.

5   Gently slip the arancini into the hot oil and fry until warmed through and golden brown, 3 to 5 minutes. Transfer the arancini to a paper towel–lined plate to drain and let them cool slightly.

6   To serve, garnish the arancini with additional Fontina and serve with Marinara Sauce.

Arancini, see page 55

TEQUILA CHEESE DIP

YIELD: **4 SERVINGS** | ACTIVE TIME: **10 MINUTES** | TOTAL TIME: **25 MINUTES**

INGREDIENTS

6 oz. Oaxaca cheese, cubed

½ plum tomato, diced

¼ white onion, diced

2 tablespoons diced green chile peppers

2 tablespoons sugar

¼ cup fresh lime juice

1 teaspoon chili powder

1 oz. tequila

1   Preheat the oven to 350°F. Place the cheese, tomato, onion, and chiles in a small cast-iron skillet and stir to combine. Set the mixture aside.

2   Combine the sugar, lime juice, and chili powder in a small saucepan and cook over medium heat, stirring to dissolve the sugar, until the mixture is syrupy.

3   Drizzle the syrup over the cheese mixture, place it in the oven, and bake until the cheese has melted and is golden brown on top, about 15 minutes.

4   Remove the pan from the oven, pour the tequila over the mixture, and use a long match or a wand lighter to ignite it. Bring the flaming skillet to the table and enjoy once the flames have gone out.

BEER CHEESE DIP

YIELD: **4 SERVINGS** | ACTIVE TIME: **20 MINUTES** | TOTAL TIME: **20 MINUTES**

INGREDIENTS

2 tablespoons unsalted butter

1½ teaspoons all-purpose flour

¾ cup brown ale

1 tablespoon Worcestershire sauce

½ teaspoon mustard powder

Pinch of cayenne pepper

1½ cups grated cheddar cheese

Salt and pepper, to taste

1 Place the butter in a saucepan and melt it over medium heat. Add the flour and cook, stirring constantly, until the mixture starts to brown, about 2 minutes.

2 Deglaze the pan with the brown ale and Worcestershire sauce, scraping up any browned bits from the bottom.

3 Add the remaining ingredients, cook until the cheese has melted, and serve immediately.

Beer Cheese Dip, see page 59

CRAB DIP

YIELD: **4 SERVINGS** | ACTIVE TIME: **15 MINUTES** | TOTAL TIME: **50 MINUTES**

INGREDIENTS

1 tablespoon unsalted butter

½ shallot, minced

¼ cup panko

Salt, to taste

1½ teaspoons dry vermouth

5 oz. cream cheese, softened

¼ cup crème fraîche

¼ cup mayonnaise

1 tablespoon Dijon mustard

¼ cup chopped fresh chives

½ lb. lump crabmeat, picked over

½ teaspoon cayenne pepper

½ teaspoon Old Bay seasoning

1 Preheat the oven to 350°F. Place the butter in a skillet and melt it over medium heat. Add the shallot and cook, stirring frequently, until it has softened, about 4 minutes.

2 Stir in the panko and cook until golden brown, 2 to 4 minutes. Remove the pan from heat.

3 Combine the panko mixture and the remaining ingredients in a mixing bowl and then transfer the mixture to a ramekin or a crock. Place the dip in the oven and bake until golden brown on top, about 35 minutes. Remove from the oven and serve immediately.

GREEN GODDESS DIP

YIELD: **6 CUPS** | ACTIVE TIME: **5 MINUTES** | TOTAL TIME: **5 MINUTES**

INGREDIENTS

1½ cups mayonnaise

2 cups sour cream

1 tablespoon chopped
fresh parsley

1 tablespoon chopped
fresh tarragon

1 tablespoon chopped
fresh chives

1 tablespoon chopped
fresh basil

1 tablespoon red wine
vinegar

1 tablespoon sugar

1 teaspoon garlic powder

1 tablespoon
Worcestershire sauce

Salt and pepper, to taste

6 oz. blue cheese

1   Place all of the ingredients, except for the blue cheese, in a food
processor and blitz until pureed.

2   Add the blue cheese and pulse a few times, making sure to maintain a
chunky texture. Store the dip in the refrigerator until ready to serve.

PESTO

YIELD: **2 CUPS** | ACTIVE TIME: **10 MINUTES** | TOTAL TIME: **10 MINUTES**

INGREDIENTS

2 cups packed fresh
basil leaves

1 cup packed fresh
baby spinach

2 cups freshly grated
Parmesan cheese

¼ cup pine nuts

1 garlic clove

2 teaspoons fresh
lemon juice

Salt and pepper, to taste

½ cup extra-virgin olive oil

1   Place all of the ingredients, except for the olive oil, in a food processor
and pulse until pureed.

2   Transfer the puree to a mixing bowl. While whisking continually, add the
olive oil in a slow stream until it is emulsified. Use immediately or store in
the refrigerator for up to 3 days.

BAKED BRIE, TWO WAYS

YIELD: **4 TO 6 SERVINGS** | ACTIVE TIME: **10 MINUTES** | TOTAL TIME: **25 MINUTES**

INGREDIENTS

8 oz. Brie cheese

For the Savory Topping

¼ cup chopped roasted tomatoes

¼ cup chopped artichoke hearts

2 tablespoons pitted and chopped olives

1 tablespoon capers

Pinch of black pepper

For the Sweet Topping

¼ cup chopped pecans

¼ cup chopped dried apricots

⅓ cup Divina fig spread

¼ cup dried cherries

Pinch of cinnamon

1 Preheat the oven to 350°F. Combine the ingredients for your chosen topping in a mixing bowl.

2 Place the Brie in a ceramic dish and top it with the chosen topping.

3 Place the dish in the oven and bake for 15 minutes, until the cheese is gooey.

4 Remove from the oven and serve.

CLASSIC FONDUE

YIELD: **6 SERVINGS** | ACTIVE TIME: **10 MINUTES** | TOTAL TIME: **20 MINUTES**

INGREDIENTS

1 lb. Gruyère cheese,
shredded

½ lb. Emmental cheese,
shredded

½ lb. gouda cheese,
shredded

2 tablespoons cornstarch

1 garlic clove, halved

1 cup white wine

1 tablespoon fresh
lemon juice

Salt and pepper, to taste

Freshly grated nutmeg,
to taste

1   Place the cheeses and the cornstarch in a bowl and toss until the cheeses are evenly coated.

2   Rub the inside of a caquelon (fondue pot) with the garlic and place the pot over the flame to warm it up.

3   Place the wine and lemon juice in a saucepan and bring the mixture to a simmer over low heat. Add the cheese mixture and cook, stirring constantly, until the cheeses have melted and the mixture is smooth. Season with salt, pepper, and nutmeg, transfer the mixture to the fondue pot, and enjoy.

FONDUE FOLKLORE

A fun fondue tradition is to leave a thin layer of fondue at the bottom of the caquelon (fondue pot). By carefully controlling the heat, you can form this layer into a crust known as La Religieuse—"The Religious One." Lift it out and distribute it among your guests. You'll see why it is considered a delicacy.

CHEESY POOFS

YIELD: **4 SERVINGS** | ACTIVE TIME: **15 MINUTES** | TOTAL TIME: **35 MINUTES**

INGREDIENTS

Canola oil, as needed

2 cups sweet potato puree

1 egg

½ cup white flour

½ teaspoon baking powder

¼ cup grated Asiago cheese

¼ cup grated Parmesan cheese

⅓ cup shredded mozzarella cheese

1   Add canola oil to a Dutch oven until it is 2 inches deep and warm it to 350°F over medium heat. Place the sweet potato puree and egg in a mixing bowl. Add the flour and baking powder and stir until the mixture is smooth.

2   Add the cheeses one at a time and fold to incorporate. Form tablespoons of the mixture into balls and gently slip them into the hot oil. Fry until they are golden brown, 4 to 6 minutes, turning them as needed.

3   Remove the cheesy poofs from the hot oil and transfer them to a paper towel-lined plate to drain and cool slightly before serving.

PARMESAN CRISPS

YIELD: **24 CRISPS** | ACTIVE TIME: **10 MINUTES** | TOTAL TIME: **25 MINUTES**

INGREDIENTS

2 cups freshly grated
Parmesan cheese

2 tablespoons Everything
Seasoning (see page 241)

2 tablespoons all-purpose
flour

1   Preheat the oven to 350°F and line a baking sheet with a Silpat mat. Place all of the ingredients in a food processor and blitz until combined.

2   Using a 2-inch ring mold, shape the mixture into rounds on the baking sheet. You want the rounds to be about ¼ inch thick.

3   Place the pan in the oven and bake until the rounds are brown and crispy, about 7 minutes. Remove the crisps from the oven and let them cool before enjoying.

POMEGRANATE-GLAZED FIGS & CHEESE

YIELD: **4 SERVINGS** | ACTIVE TIME: **35 MINUTES** | TOTAL TIME: **1 HOUR**

INGREDIENTS

2 cups pomegranate juice

1 teaspoon fennel seeds

1 teaspoon black peppercorns

1 bay leaf

Pinch of kosher salt, plus more to taste

½ cup ricotta cheese

½ cup mascarpone cheese

⅛ teaspoon freshly ground black pepper

12 fresh figs

1 teaspoon caster sugar (superfine)

Pomegranate seeds, for garnish

1 Place the pomegranate juice, fennel seeds, peppercorns, bay leaf, and salt in a small saucepan and simmer the mixture over medium-high heat until it has been reduced to ⅓ cup.

2 Strain and let the glaze cool completely.

3 In a bowl, combine the cheeses. Add 1 tablespoon of the glaze and season the mixture with salt and the pepper. Place the mixture in a pastry bag that has been fitted with a plain ½-inch tip and set it aside.

4 Preheat the broiler on the oven. Cut the figs in half from tip to stem and place them in a heatproof dish, cut side up. Brush the cut sides with some of the glaze and dust with the caster sugar.

5 Pipe a ½-inch-wide and 6-inch-long strip of the cheese mixture on four plates.

6 Place the figs under the broiler until glazed and just warmed through, about 5 minutes.

7 To serve, arrange six fig halves on top of each strip of cheese, garnish with pomegranate seeds, and drizzle any remaining glaze over the top.

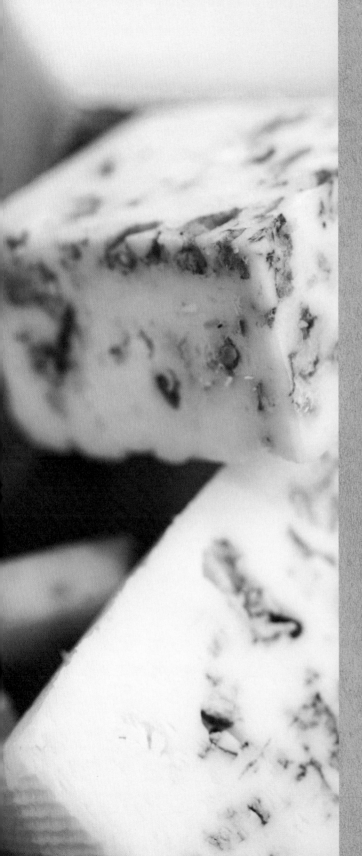

As this is a cookbook, it's focused on those recipes that make the most of cheese's numerous talents. But we'd be remiss if we didn't take a moment to touch on one of the very best ways to express your love for cheese: on a board, accompanied by crackers or crusty bread, fruit, nuts, and/or olives, a glass of wine, and some pleasant conversation. If that simple scene is calling to you, here are a few tips to keep in mind:

Cut or crumble hard cheeses so that they are more approachable. With softer cheeses, leave them whole or halved for scooping and spreading. Everyone loves seeing the insides of softer cheeses, so cut the wheels in half the way you would slice a bagel.

Always serve your cheese at room temperature so that it really shines.

Always include one familiar cheese, like a cheddar, so that your guests immediately feel comfortable diving in. After a glass of wine or two, you will find that your guests tend to get a bit more adventurous.

Create variety by choosing cheeses from different categories, such as fresh, soft, semi-soft, hard, or blue. Another way of creating variety is by selecting your cheeses based on the type of milk they are made from. For a winning board, don't hesitate to use cheeses made from the milk of cows, goats, and sheep.

MARINATED FETA

YIELD: **4 SERVINGS** | ACTIVE TIME: **5 MINUTES** | TOTAL TIME: **2 HOURS AND 5 MINUTES**

INGREDIENTS

½ lb. feta cheese

1 sprig of fresh basil

¾ cup extra-virgin olive oil

½ cup white wine vinegar

2 tablespoons black pepper

1 teaspoon kosher salt

¾ teaspoon red pepper flakes

1   Cut the feta into bite-size chunks and place them in a mason jar.

2   Combine the remaining ingredients in a mixing bowl and then pour the marinade over the feta. Let it marinate for at least 2 hours before enjoying.

GRILLED HALLOUMI

YIELD: **4 SERVINGS** | ACTIVE TIME: **5 MINUTES** | TOTAL TIME: **20 MINUTES**

INGREDIENTS

½ lb. halloumi cheese

Extra-virgin olive oil, to taste

1   Preheat a gas or charcoal grill to 350°F. Cut the halloumi into pieces that are approximately ½ inch wide.

2   Drizzle olive oil over the cheese and place it on the grill. Grill until the cheese is warm and has grill marks on both sides, about 6 minutes. Remove from the grill and serve immediately.

Grilled Halloumi, see page 79

BAKED CAMEMBERT

YIELD: **4 SERVINGS** | ACTIVE TIME: **5 MINUTES** | TOTAL TIME: **25 MINUTES**

INGREDIENTS

½ lb. round of Camembert cheese

1 cup granola

½ cup real maple syrup

1   Preheat the oven to 350°F. Place the Camembert in a small cast-iron skillet or a ceramic dish. Sprinkle the granola over the cheese and drizzle the maple syrup on top.

2   Place in the oven and bake until the cheese is gooey, about 15 minutes. Remove from the oven and serve immediately.

ROASTED CAULIFLOWER AU GRATIN

YIELD: **2 SERVINGS** | ACTIVE TIME: **20 MINUTES** | TOTAL TIME: **1 HOUR AND 15 MINUTES**

INGREDIENTS

2 cups white wine

2½ cups water

⅓ cup kosher salt

½ lb. unsalted butter

6 garlic cloves, crushed

2 shallots, halved

1 cinnamon stick

3 whole cloves

1 teaspoon black peppercorns

1 sprig of fresh sage

2 sprigs of fresh thyme

1 head of cauliflower, leaves and stalk removed

1 cup shredded Swiss cheese

¼ cup grated Parmesan cheese

1   Place all of the ingredients, except for the cauliflower and cheeses, in a large saucepan and bring to a boil. Reduce the heat so that the mixture simmers gently, add the head of cauliflower, and poach until it is tender, about 30 minutes.

2   While the cauliflower is poaching, preheat the oven to 450°F. Transfer the tender cauliflower to a baking sheet, place it in the oven, and bake until the top is a deep golden brown, about 10 minutes.

3   Remove the cauliflower from the oven and spread the cheeses evenly over the top. Return to the oven and bake until the cheeses have browned. Remove the cauliflower from the oven and let cool slightly before cutting the cauliflower in half and serving.

CHEESY HASH BROWNS

YIELD: **4 TO 6 SERVINGS** | ACTIVE TIME: **20 MINUTES** | TOTAL TIME: **1 HOUR**

INGREDIENTS

4 large russet potatoes, peeled and shredded

4 tablespoons unsalted butter

1 teaspoon kosher salt

Black pepper, to taste

6 eggs

½ cup milk

1 cup shredded cheddar cheese

1   Preheat the oven to 375°F. Place the potatoes in a linen towel and wring the towel to remove as much moisture from the potatoes as possible. Place the potatoes in a bowl.

2   Place the butter in a large cast-iron skillet and melt it over medium-high heat. Add the potatoes and salt and season with pepper. Press down on the potatoes to ensure they are in an even layer. Cook the potatoes, without stirring, for 5 minutes.

3   In a mixing bowl, whisk the eggs and milk until combined. Pour the mixture over the potatoes and shake the pan to help the egg mixture penetrate to the bottom. Sprinkle the cheese on top and then transfer the skillet to the oven.

4   Bake until the cheese is melted and golden brown, about 10 minutes. Remove the skillet from the oven and enjoy.

SQUASH & FETA SALAD

YIELD: **4 SERVINGS** | ACTIVE TIME: **15 MINUTES** | TOTAL TIME: **40 MINUTES**

INGREDIENTS

1½ lb. acorn squash

1½ teaspoons kosher salt

¼ teaspoon black pepper

½ cup avocado oil

4 cups cubed French bread

½ lb. feta cheese, crumbled

¼ cup sherry vinegar

1 teaspoon honey

1 teaspoon fresh thyme

½ teaspoon sweet Hungarian paprika

½ teaspoon cayenne pepper

1 head of radicchio, leaves separated and torn

1 Preheat the oven to 400°F. Halve the squash lengthwise, remove the seeds and reserve them for another preparation, and cut the squash into ¼-inch-thick slices.

2 Place the squash on a baking sheet, season it with 1 teaspoon of the salt and the black pepper, drizzle 2 tablespoons of the avocado oil over it, and toss to coat. Place the squash in the oven and roast until it is beginning to brown on one side, about 15 minutes.

3 Remove the baking sheet from the oven, turn the squash over, and then sprinkle the bread and feta over the squash. Return the pan to the oven and roast until the bread is lightly toasted and the feta is soft and warmed through, about 10 minutes.

4 Place the vinegar, honey, thyme, remaining avocado oil, and remaining salt in a large bowl and whisk until thoroughly combined.

5 In a small bowl, combine the paprika and cayenne and set the mixture aside.

6 Add the radicchio and warm squash mixture to the dressing and toss to coat.

7 Transfer to a serving dish, sprinkle the paprika-and-cayenne blend over the dish, and enjoy.

STRAWBERRY & BEET SALAD

YIELD: **4 SERVINGS** | ACTIVE TIME: **20 MINUTES** | TOTAL TIME: **2 HOURS**

INGREDIENTS

3 large golden beets

½ cup extra-virgin olive oil

Salt and pepper, to taste

Cilantro Pesto (see page 242)

12 strawberries, hulled and halved

2 cups shredded queso fresco

4 oz. baby arugula

2 tablespoons annatto oil

1   Preheat the oven to 375°F. Rinse the beets under cold water and scrub them to remove any excess dirt. Pat dry and place them in a baking dish.

2   Drizzle the olive oil over the beets and season them generously with salt and pepper. Place them in the oven and roast until tender, about 1 hour.

3   Remove the beets from the oven and let them cool.

4   When the beets are cool enough to handle, peel and dice them. Place them in a bowl with the pesto and toss to coat. Add the strawberries, cheese, arugula, and annatto oil, toss until evenly distributed, and serve.

Strawberry & Beet Salad, see page 89

ROASTED BRUSSELS SPROUTS WITH BLUE CHEESE

YIELD: **4 SERVINGS** | ACTIVE TIME: **30 MINUTES** | TOTAL TIME: **2 HOURS**

INGREDIENTS

1 cup champagne vinegar

1 cup water

½ cup sugar

2 teaspoons kosher salt, plus more to taste

1 small red onion, sliced

½ lb. bacon, cut into 1-inch pieces

1½ lbs. Brussels sprouts, trimmed and halved

Black pepper, to taste

4 oz. blue cheese, crumbled

1   Place the vinegar, water, sugar, and salt in a saucepan and bring the mixture to a boil. Place the onion in a bowl and pour the boiling liquid over it. Cover the bowl with plastic wrap and let the mixture cool completely.

2   Place the bacon in a large skillet and cook it over medium heat, stirring occasionally, until the bacon is crispy, about 8 minutes. Transfer the bacon to a paper towel–lined plate to drain and leave the rendered fat in the pan.

3   Place the Brussels sprouts in the pan, cut side down, season them with salt and pepper, and cook over medium heat until they are a deep golden brown all over, about 7 minutes, turning them as necessary.

4   Transfer the Brussels sprouts to a platter, top with the pickled red onion, bacon, and blue cheese, and enjoy.

ESQUITES

YIELD: **4 SERVINGS** | ACTIVE TIME: **5 MINUTES** | TOTAL TIME: **5 MINUTES**

INGREDIENTS

4 cups canned corn, drained

2 tablespoons unsalted butter

1 jalapeño chile pepper, stem and seeds removed, diced

2 tablespoons mayonnaise

2 teaspoons garlic powder

3 tablespoons sour cream

¼ teaspoon cayenne pepper

¼ teaspoon chili powder

4 oz. goat cheese, crumbled

2 teaspoons fresh lime juice

½ cup finely chopped fresh cilantro

Salt and pepper, to taste

4 cups lettuce or arugula

1   Place the corn in a large mixing bowl.

2   Add the remaining ingredients one at a time, stirring until each one has been thoroughly incorporated before adding the next.

3   Taste, adjust the seasoning as necessary, and enjoy.

WATERMELON & RICOTTA SALAD

YIELD: **4 SERVINGS** | ACTIVE TIME: **10 MINUTES** | TOTAL TIME: **15 MINUTES**

INGREDIENTS

4 cups arugula

2 tablespoons extra-virgin olive oil

Flesh of 1 large watermelon, cubed

1 cup ricotta cheese

Fresh cracked black pepper, to taste

1 Place the arugula in a salad bowl. Add the olive oil and toss to combine.

2 Divide the watermelon among four bowls and top each of them with a generous scoop of ricotta.

3 Add the dressed arugula, season with black pepper, and serve.

CHARRED BRASSICA SALAD WITH BUTTERMILK CAESAR

YIELD: **4 SERVINGS** | ACTIVE TIME: **20 MINUTES** | TOTAL TIME: **45 MINUTES**

1   To begin preparations for the salad, bring a large pot of water to a boil. Add salt and the cauliflower, cook for 1 minute, remove the cauliflower with a slotted spoon, and transfer to a paper towel–lined plate. Wait for the water to return to a boil, add the broccoli, and cook for 30 seconds. Use a slotted spoon to remove the broccoli and transfer it to the paper towel–lined plate.

2   Place the oil and Brussels sprouts, cut side down, in a large cast-iron skillet. Add the broccoli and cauliflower, season with salt and pepper, and cook over high heat, making sure not to stir the vegetables, until they start to char. Turn the vegetables over and cook until lightly charred on that side. Remove the mixture from the pan and transfer it to a salad bowl.

3   To prepare the dressing, place the garlic, miso, mayonnaise, buttermilk, Parmesan, lemon zest, Worcestershire sauce, salt, and pepper in a food processor and blitz until combined. Taste and adjust the seasoning if necessary.

4   Add the Pickled Ramps and dressing to the salad bowl and toss to coat. Garnish with Parmesan and red pepper flakes and serve.

INGREDIENTS

For the Salad

Salt and pepper, to taste

1 small head of cauliflower, trimmed and chopped

1 head of broccoli, cut into florets

¼ cup extra-virgin olive oil

4 oz. Brussels sprouts, trimmed and halved

Pickled Ramps (see page 235)

Parmesan cheese, grated, for garnish

Red pepper flakes, for garnish

For the Dressing

2 garlic cloves, minced

1 teaspoon miso paste

⅔ cup mayonnaise

¼ cup buttermilk

¼ cup grated Parmesan cheese

Zest of 1 lemon

1 teaspoon Worcestershire sauce

1 teaspoon kosher salt

½ teaspoon black pepper

CHEDDAR & JALAPEÑO SCONES

YIELD: **4 TO 6 SERVINGS** | ACTIVE TIME: **30 MINUTES** | TOTAL TIME: **50 MINUTES**

INGREDIENTS

2 cups all-purpose flour, plus more for dusting

1 teaspoon baking powder

½ teaspoon fine sea salt

1 teaspoon black pepper

4 tablespoons unsalted butter, chilled, cut into small pieces

¾ cup grated sharp cheddar cheese

½ cup sliced or chopped jalapeño pepper

½ cup whole milk

1 egg, beaten

1   Preheat the oven to 400°F. Position a rack in the middle of the oven.

2   In a mixing bowl, whisk together the flour, baking powder, salt, and black pepper. Add the butter pieces and work the mixture with a pastry cutter until it comes together as a crumbly dough.

3   Stir in the cheese, jalapeño, and milk, being careful not to overwork the dough.

4   With flour-dusted hands, transfer the dough to a lightly floured surface. Form the dough into a circle that is about ½ inch thick. With a long knife, cut the dough into 12 wedges.

5   Place the wedges in a circle in a lightly greased 12-inch cast-iron skillet, leaving some space between the pieces.

6   Brush the scones with the beaten egg and place them in the oven. Bake the scones until they are golden brown on top, about 25 minutes.

7   Remove the scones from the oven and let them cool slightly before enjoying.

CHEESY SODA BREAD WITH CHIVES

YIELD: **1 LOAF** | ACTIVE TIME: **40 MINUTES** | TOTAL TIME: **1 HOUR AND 45 MINUTES**

INGREDIENTS

3 cups all-purpose flour

2 cups spelt flour

¾ cup old-fashioned rolled oats

2 tablespoons sugar

1 tablespoon baking powder

1 teaspoon fine sea salt

1 teaspoon baking soda

½ cup unsalted butter, melted and cooled, plus more as needed

2½ cups buttermilk

1 large egg, lightly beaten

¼ cup chopped chives

1¼ cups grated sharp white cheddar cheese

Black pepper, to taste

1   Preheat the oven to 350°F. In the work bowl of a stand mixer fitted with the paddle attachment, combine the flours, oats, sugar, baking powder, salt, and baking soda. In another bowl, combine the butter, buttermilk, and egg.

2   Add the buttermilk mixture to the flour mixture and beat the mixture until it comes together as a sticky dough. Stir in the chives and 1 cup of the grated cheese.

3   Generously coat a 12-inch cast-iron skillet with butter. Place the dough in the skillet, making sure to spread it into an even layer. Sprinkle black pepper over the dough, and then sprinkle the remaining cheese over the top. Using a sharp knife, make an x in the center of the dough, about ½ inch deep, so that the cheese can settle into the dough as the bread cooks.

4   Place the pan in the oven and bake the bread until it is golden brown on top and a toothpick inserted into the center comes out clean, about 1 hour.

5   Remove the bread from the oven and let it rest in the pan for a few minutes before enjoying.

BEER & CHEESE BREAD

YIELD: **1 LOAF** | ACTIVE TIME: **15 MINUTES** | TOTAL TIME: **1 HOUR AND 15 MINUTES**

INGREDIENTS

1 tablespoon unsalted butter, melted

3 cups all-purpose flour

1 cup chopped green onions

3 tablespoons sugar

4 teaspoons baking powder

1½ teaspoons fine sea salt

1 tablespoon dried parsley

2 cups grated cheddar cheese

1½ cups lager or lighter ale

1   Preheat the oven to 400°F and lightly coat a 10-inch cast-iron skillet with the melted butter.

2   Place the flour, green onions, sugar, baking powder, salt, and dried parsley in a large bowl and stir to combine. Add the cheese and stir to incorporate, making sure it is coated with flour and not clumped together.

3   Add the beer and stir until the mixture just comes together as a dough, taking care to not overwork the mixture.

4   Pour the dough into the greased skillet and smooth the top with a rubber spatula. Place the pan in the oven and bake until it is golden brown, about 30 minutes, rotating the pan once or twice as the bread bakes.

5   Remove the pan from the oven and let the bread cool for 30 minutes before slicing.

PÃO DE QUEIJO

YIELD: **12 BUNS** | ACTIVE TIME: **20 MINUTES** | TOTAL TIME: **45 MINUTES**

INGREDIENTS

11 oz. tapioca starch

1 cup milk

½ cup unsalted butter

1 teaspoon kosher salt

2 eggs

1½ cups grated Parmesan cheese

1   Preheat the oven to 350°F. Line an 18 x 13–inch baking sheet with parchment paper. Place the tapioca starch in the work bowl of a stand mixer fitted with the paddle attachment.

2   Place the milk, butter, and salt in a small saucepan and warm over medium heat until the butter has melted and the mixture is simmering.

3   Turn the mixer on low and slowly pour the milk mixture into the work bowl. Raise the speed to medium and work the mixture until it has cooled considerably.

4   Add the eggs one at a time and knead to incorporate. Add the grated cheese and knead the mixture until incorporated.

5   Scoop twelve 2-oz. portions of the dough onto the pan, making sure to leave enough space between them.

6   Place the pan in the oven and bake until the buns are puffy and light golden brown, 15 to 20 minutes.

7   Remove the buns from the oven and enjoy immediately.

JALAPEÑO & CHEDDAR CORNBREAD

YIELD: **12 SERVINGS** | ACTIVE TIME: **20 MINUTES** | TOTAL TIME: **1 HOUR**

INGREDIENTS

1 lb. all-purpose flour

½ lb. cornmeal

1 tablespoon plus 1 teaspoon baking powder

1 tablespoon kosher salt

3 jalapeño chile peppers, stems and seeds removed, diced

2 cups shredded cheddar cheese

1 cup unsalted butter, softened

7 oz. sugar

4 eggs

2 cups milk

1 Preheat the oven to 350°F. Coat a 13 x 9–inch baking pan with nonstick cooking spray.

2 Place the flour, cornmeal, baking powder, salt, jalapeños, and cheese in a mixing bowl and whisk to combine. Set the mixture aside.

3 In the work bowl of a stand mixer fitted with the paddle attachment, cream the butter and sugar on medium until light and fluffy, about 5 minutes. Add the eggs and beat until incorporated. Add the dry mixture, reduce the speed to low, and beat until the mixture comes together as a smooth batter. Gradually add the milk and beat until incorporated.

4 Pour the batter into the pan, place the pan in the oven, and bake until a cake tester inserted into the center of the cornbread comes out clean, 25 to 30 minutes.

5 Remove from the oven and place the pan on a wire rack. Let the cornbread cool slightly before slicing and serving.

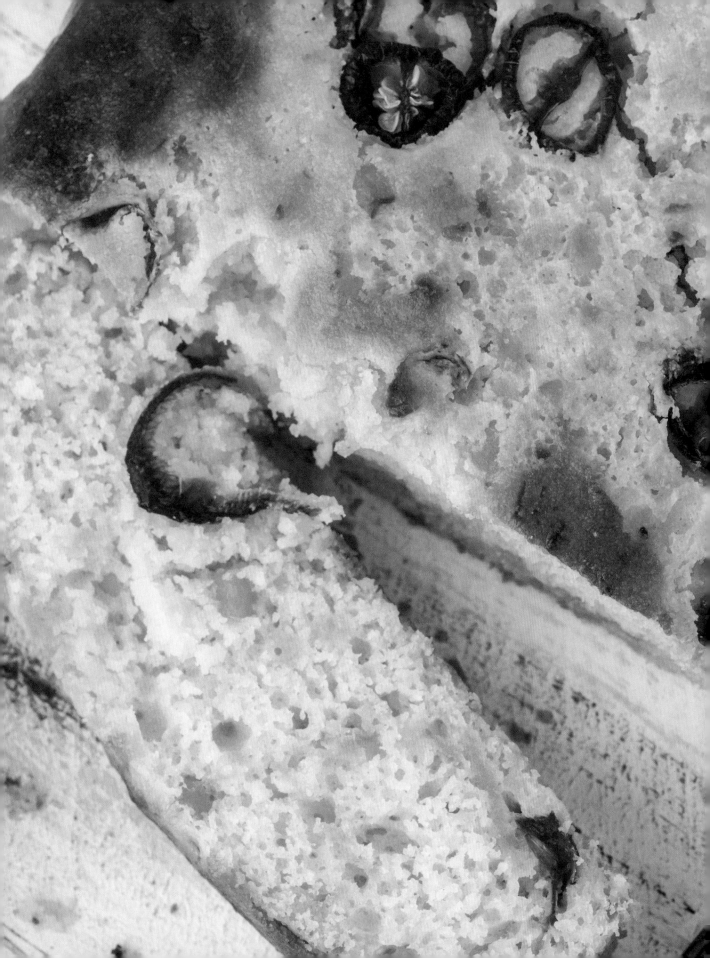

ENTREES

When a craving for something cheesy hits, chances are one of the preparations in this chapter is what comes to mind. Whether you want the quick comfort of a grilled cheese, the rustic complexity of French onion soup, the silky decadence of fettuccine alfredo, or the unparalleled indulgence of pizza, a salve can be found in the following pages.

NEW YORK-STYLE PIZZA

YIELD: **2 PIZZAS** | ACTIVE TIME: **45 MINUTES** | TOTAL TIME: **9 HOURS**

INGREDIENTS

⅛ teaspoon instant yeast

10.9 oz. bread flour or "00" flour, plus more as needed

6¾ oz. water

1½ teaspoons fine sea salt

Extra-virgin olive oil, as needed

Semolina flour, as needed

1 cup Marinara Sauce (see page 245)

3 cups shredded mozzarella cheese

Dried oregano, to taste

1 In a large bowl, combine the yeast, flour, and water. Work the mixture until it just holds together. Dust a work surface with either bread or "00" flour and knead the dough until it is compact, smooth, and elastic.

2 Add the salt and knead until the dough is developed and elastic, meaning it pulls back when stretched. Transfer the dough to an airtight container and let it rest at room temperature for 2 hours.

3 Divide the dough into two pieces and shape them into very tight balls. Place the balls of dough in a baking dish with high edges, leaving enough space between rounds that they won't touch when fully risen. Cover with oiled plastic wrap and let them rest until they have doubled in size, about 6 hours.

4 Place a baking stone on the middle rack of your oven and preheat the oven to the maximum temperature. Dust a work surface with semolina flour, place the balls of dough on the surface, and gently stretch them into 10- to 12-inch rounds. Cover them with the sauce and top with the mozzarella. Season with oregano and drizzle olive oil over the pizzas.

5 Using a peel or a flat baking sheet, transfer one pizza at a time to the heated baking stone in the oven. Bake for about 15 minutes, until the crust is golden brown and starting to char. Remove, repeat with the other pizza, and let both cool slightly before serving.

STEAK & PEARL ONION FRITTATA

YIELD: **6 SERVINGS** | ACTIVE TIME: **10 MINUTES** | TOTAL TIME: **25 MINUTES**

INGREDIENTS

2 tablespoons extra-virgin olive oil

1 lb. pearl onions

Salt and pepper, to taste

12 large eggs

½ cup heavy cream

½ lb. strip steak, minced

4 tablespoons unsalted butter

2 tablespoons chopped fresh parsley

2 cups grated Parmesan cheese

1   Preheat the oven to 400°F. Place a 10-inch cast-iron skillet over medium-high heat and add the olive oil. Add the pearl onions, salt, and pepper and cook until the onions start to caramelize, 5 to 7 minutes.

2   While the onions are cooking, place the eggs, cream, salt, and pepper in a bowl and scramble until combined.

3   Add the steak to the skillet and cook, stirring occasionally, until it is cooked through, 4 to 6 minutes. Stir in the butter and parsley, sprinkle the cheese evenly over the mixture, then pour the egg mixture into the pan, gently shaking the skillet to make sure the egg mixture gets evenly distributed.

4   Place the skillet in the oven and cook for 8 minutes. Turn the oven's broiler on and cook until the top of the frittata is browned, 3 to 4 minutes. Remove the frittata from the oven and let it rest for 10 minutes before serving.

CHILES EN NOGADA

YIELD: **4 SERVINGS** | ACTIVE TIME: **45 MINUTES** | TOTAL TIME: **1 HOUR AND 15 MINUTES**

INGREDIENTS

4 poblano chile peppers

1 cup almonds or walnuts

¼ cup crumbled queso fresco

2 cups sour cream, plus more as needed

½ tablespoon sugar

Salt, to taste

3 cups Picadillo de Res (see page 237), at room temperature

¼ cup pomegranate seeds, for garnish

Fresh cilantro, chopped, for garnish

1   If you do not have a gas stove, preheat a grill or the oven to 400°F. Roast the poblanos over an open flame, on the grill, or in the oven until the skin is blackened and blistered all over, turning occasionally. Place the poblanos in a heatproof bowl, cover with plastic wrap, and let sit for 10 minutes.

2   Remove the charred skins from the poblanos. Make a small slit in the peppers and remove the seeds.

3   Place the nuts, queso fresco, sour cream, and sugar in a blender and puree until smooth. If the sauce seems too thick, incorporate more sour cream until the sauce is the desired texture. Season the sauce with salt and set it aside.

4   Stuff the peppers with the picadillo.

5   To serve, spoon the sauce over the peppers and garnish with the pomegranate seeds and cilantro.

Chiles en Nogada, see page 113

COUSCOUS & SHRIMP SALAD

YIELD: **6 SERVINGS** | ACTIVE TIME: **40 MINUTES** | TOTAL TIME: **50 MINUTES**

INGREDIENTS

¾ lb. shrimp, shells removed, deveined

6 bunches of fresh mint

10 garlic cloves, peeled

3½ cups Chicken Stock (see page 239)

3 cups Israeli couscous

1 bunch of asparagus, trimmed

3 plum tomatoes, diced

1 tablespoon finely chopped fresh oregano

½ English cucumber, diced

Zest and juice of 1 lemon

½ cup diced red onion

½ cup sun-dried tomatoes in olive oil, sliced thin

¼ cup pitted and chopped Kalamata olives

⅓ cup olive oil

Salt and pepper, to taste

½ cup crumbled feta cheese

1   Place the shrimp, mint, and garlic in a Dutch oven and cover with water. Bring to a simmer over medium heat and cook until the shrimp are pink and cooked through, about 5 minutes after the water comes to a simmer. Drain, cut the shrimp in half lengthwise, and them set aside. Discard the mint and garlic cloves.

2   Place the stock in the Dutch oven and bring to a boil. Add the couscous, reduce the heat so that the stock simmers, cover, and cook until the couscous is tender and has absorbed the stock, 7 to 10 minutes. Transfer the couscous to a salad bowl.

3   Fill the pot with water and bring it to a boil. Add the asparagus and cook until it has softened, 1 to 1½ minutes. Drain, rinse under cold water, and chop into bite-size pieces. Pat the asparagus dry.

4   Add all of the remaining ingredients, except for the feta, to the salad bowl containing the couscous. Add the asparagus and stir to incorporate. Top with the shrimp and feta and serve.

BEEF & PORK CHEESEBURGERS WITH CARAMELIZED ONION MAYONNAISE

YIELD: **6 SERVINGS** | ACTIVE TIME: **40 MINUTES** | TOTAL TIME: **3 HOURS AND 30 MINUTES**

INGREDIENTS

1 lb. ground beef

1 lb. ground pork

Salt and pepper, to taste

2 tablespoons unsalted butter

2 sweet onions, sliced thin

½ cup mayonnaise

6 brioche buns, toasted

6 slices of cheddar cheese

1   Place the beef and pork in a mixing bowl and season the mixture with salt and pepper. Stir to combine, cover the bowl with plastic wrap, and place it in the refrigerator.

2   Place the butter in a skillet and melt it over medium-low heat.

3   Add the onions and a pinch of salt and cook, stirring frequently, until the onions develop a deep brown color, 20 to 30 minutes. Remove the pan from heat and let the onions cool completely.

4   Transfer the cooled onions to a food processor and blitz until smooth. Place the puree and mayonnaise in a mixing bowl, season the mixture with salt and pepper, and stir to combine. Chill the mixture in the refrigerator for 2 hours.

5   When ready to serve, prepare a gas or charcoal grill for medium-high heat (about 450°F) or place a cast-iron skillet over medium-high heat. Divide the beef-and-pork mixture into 6 balls and then gently shape them into patties.

6   Place the burgers on the grill or in the skillet and cook for 8 to 10 minutes. Flip the burgers over and cook until cooked through, about 5 to 8 minutes. Since you are working with pork, it is important to cook the burgers all the way through. If you're worried that they will dry out, don't fret. The pork fat will keep the burgers moist and flavorful.

7   Spread the mayonnaise on the bottoms of the buns. Place a burger on the other halves of the buns, top them with the slices of cheese, assemble the burgers, and enjoy.

MAC & CHEESE WITH BROWN BUTTER BREAD CRUMBS

YIELD: **6 SERVINGS** | ACTIVE TIME: **30 MINUTES** | TOTAL TIME: **1 HOUR**

INGREDIENTS

Salt, to taste

1 lb. elbow macaroni

7 tablespoons unsalted butter

2 cups panko

½ yellow onion, minced

3 tablespoons all-purpose flour

1 tablespoon yellow mustard

1 teaspoon turmeric

1 teaspoon garlic powder

1 teaspoon white pepper

2 cups light cream

2 cups whole milk

1 lb. American cheese, sliced

10 oz. Boursin cheese

½ lb. extra-sharp cheddar cheese, sliced

1   Preheat the oven to 400°F. Fill a Dutch oven with water and bring it to a boil. Add salt and the macaroni and cook until the macaroni is just shy of al dente, about 6 minutes. Drain and set aside.

2   Place the pot over medium heat and add 3 tablespoons of the butter. Cook until the butter starts to brown and give off a nutty aroma. Add the panko, stir, and cook until the bread crumbs start to look like wet sand, about 4 minutes. Remove the bread crumbs from the pot and set them aside.

3   Wipe out the Dutch oven, place it over medium-high heat, and add the onion and remaining butter. Cook, stirring occasionally, until the onion is soft, about 10 minutes. Gradually add the flour, stirring constantly to prevent lumps from forming. Stir in the mustard, turmeric, garlic powder, white pepper, cream, and milk, reduce the heat to medium, and bring the mixture to a simmer.

4   Add the cheeses one at a time, stirring to incorporate before adding the next one. When all of the cheeses have been incorporated and the mixture is smooth, cook the mixture until the flour taste is completely gone, about 10 minutes. Stir in the macaroni and top the mixture with the bread crumbs.

5   Place the Dutch oven in the oven and bake until the bread crumbs are crispy, 10 to 15 minutes. Remove from the oven and serve immediately.

CHIPOTLE CHICKEN ENCHILADAS

YIELD: **4 SERVINGS** | ACTIVE TIME: **25 MINUTES** | TOTAL TIME: **1 HOUR AND 30 MINUTES**

1   To prepare the sauce, bring water to a boil in a small saucepan. Add the chipotles and cook until they are rehydrated, about 10 minutes. Drain and transfer the chipotles to a food processor. Add the remaining ingredients and blitz until smooth. Add the puree to a large skillet and cook over medium-low heat until the sauce is thick enough to coat the back of a wooden spoon, 15 to 20 minutes. Remove the sauce from the pan and set it aside.

2   To begin preparations for the enchiladas, place a large cast-iron skillet over medium-high heat and warm 2 tablespoons of the olive oil in it. Season the chicken with salt and pepper and add it to the pan. Sear the chicken on both sides and then add 1½ cups of the stock. Cover and cook until the chicken is tender enough to shred with a fork, about 20 minutes. Remove the chicken, transfer it to a mixing bowl, and shred it with two forks.

3   Add the remaining olive oil and the potatoes to the skillet. Cook, stirring occasionally, until the potatoes are browned, about 5 minutes. Add the onion and garlic and cook, stirring frequently, until the onion starts to soften, about 5 minutes.

4   Reduce the heat to medium and stir in the shredded chicken, the remaining stock, the green chilies, and 1 tablespoon of the sauce. Cook until the stock has evaporated, 5 to 10 minutes. Remove the mixture from the pan and set it aside.

5   Preheat the oven to 375°F and coat a 13 x 9–inch baking pan with nonstick cooking spray. Place the tortillas on the counter and spread a small amount of sauce on each one. Divide the filling among the tortillas and roll them up. Place the tortillas, seam side down, in the baking pan.

6   Top the enchiladas with the remaining sauce and place the pan in the oven. Bake until a crust forms on the exterior of the tortillas, about 20 minutes.

7   Remove the enchiladas from the oven, garnish with the Cotija and cilantro, and enjoy.

INGREDIENTS

For the Sauce

4 dried chipotle chile peppers

½ (7 oz.) can of diced green chilies

2 tablespoons extra-virgin olive oil

3 plum tomatoes, seeded

1 tablespoon tomato paste

1 tablespoon cumin

1 teaspoon dried oregano

Salt and pepper, to taste

For the Enchiladas

¼ cup extra-virgin olive oil

6 boneless, skinless chicken thighs

Salt and pepper, to taste

2 cups Chicken Stock (see page 239)

2 russet potatoes, peeled and minced

½ white onion, minced

2 garlic cloves, minced

½ (7 oz.) can of diced mild green chilies

24 Corn Tortillas (see page 243)

½ cup crumbled Cotija cheese, for garnish

Fresh cilantro, finely chopped, for garnish

CHICKEN & TOMATILLO CASSEROLE

YIELD: **6 SERVINGS** | ACTIVE TIME: **15 MINUTES** | TOTAL TIME: **24 HOURS**

INGREDIENTS

For the Marinade

1 tomatillo, husked, rinsed, and halved

1 plum tomato, halved

2 garlic cloves, crushed

1 shallot, halved

1 poblano pepper, stem and seeds removed, halved

¼ cup extra-virgin olive oil

1 tablespoon kosher salt

1 tablespoon cumin

For the Casserole

2 lbs. boneless, skinless chicken breasts, sliced thin

2 eggs, beaten

1 (14 oz.) can of fire-roasted tomatoes, drained

Pinch of kosher salt

14 Corn Tortillas (see page 243)

1 cup Salsa Verde (see page 246)

¼ cup crumbled Cotija cheese

1   To prepare the marinade, place all of the ingredients in a blender and puree until the mixture is smooth.

2   To begin preparations for the casserole, place the chicken breasts in a large baking pan or resealable plastic bag. Pour the marinade over the chicken and let it marinate in the refrigerator overnight.

3   Preheat the oven to 375°F. Place the chicken and marinade in a square 8-inch baking dish, place it in the oven, and roast until the center of the chicken reaches 165°F, about 30 minutes. Remove the dish from the oven, remove the chicken, transfer it to a mixing bowl, and shred it with a fork. Add the eggs, tomatoes, and salt to the bowl and stir to combine.

4   Place four of the tortillas in the baking dish. Add half of the chicken mixture, top with four more tortillas, and add the remaining chicken mixture. Top with the remaining tortillas, cover with the salsa, and then place the dish in the oven.

5   Bake the casserole until the center is hot, about 30 minutes. Remove the casserole from the oven, sprinkle the cheese over the top, and return the casserole to the oven.

6   Bake until the cheese has melted, remove the casserole from the oven, and let it cool slightly before enjoying.

FRENCH ONION SOUP

YIELD: **6 SERVINGS** | ACTIVE TIME: **1 HOUR** | TOTAL TIME: **2 HOURS AND 30 MINUTES**

INGREDIENTS

3 tablespoons unsalted butter

7 large sweet onions, sliced

2 teaspoons kosher salt

⅓ cup orange juice

3 oz. sherry

3 tablespoons fresh thyme

7 cups Beef Stock (see page 238)

3 garlic cloves, minced

2 teaspoons black pepper

6 slices of day-old bread

1 cup shredded Gruyère cheese

1 cup shredded Emmental cheese

1 Place the butter, onions, and salt in a Dutch oven and cook the mixture over low heat, stirring frequently, until the onions are dark brown and caramelized, 40 minutes to 1 hour.

2 Deglaze the pot with the orange juice and sherry, using a wooden spoon to scrape any browned bits from the bottom of the pot. Add the thyme, stock, garlic, and pepper, raise the heat to medium, and bring to a simmer. Simmer for 1 hour.

3 While the soup is simmering, preheat the oven to 450°F.

4 After 1 hour, ladle the soup into oven-safe crocks or bowls and place a slice of bread on top of each portion. Sprinkle the cheeses over each portion, place the crocks in the oven, and bake until the cheese begins to brown, about 10 minutes. Carefully remove the bowls from the oven and let the soup cool for 10 minutes before serving.

MOUSSAKA

YIELD: **4 SERVINGS** | ACTIVE TIME: **1 HOUR AND 15 MINUTES** | TOTAL TIME: **2 HOURS**

1   Preheat the oven to 350°F. To begin preparations for the filling, place the cold water in a bowl, add the salt, and stir. When the salt has dissolved, add the eggplant cubes and let the cubes soak for about 20 minutes. Drain the eggplants and rinse with cold water. Squeeze the cubes to remove as much water as you can, place them on a pile of paper towels, and blot them dry. Set the eggplants aside.

2   Add a tablespoon of the olive oil to a large cast-iron skillet and warm it over medium-high heat. When the oil starts to shimmer, add the ground lamb and cook, using a wooden spoon to break it up, until it is browned, about 8 minutes. Transfer the cooked lamb to a bowl and set it aside.

3   Add 2 tablespoons of the olive oil and the eggplant cubes to the skillet and cook, stirring frequently, until they start to brown, about 5 minutes. Transfer the cooked eggplants to the bowl containing the lamb and add the rest of the oil, the onions, and the garlic to the skillet. Cook, stirring frequently, until the onions are translucent, about 3 minutes. Return the lamb and eggplants to the skillet, and stir in the wine, sauce, parsley, oregano, and cinnamon. Reduce the heat to low and simmer for about 15 minutes, stirring occasionally. Season with salt, pepper, and nutmeg and transfer the mixture to a 13 x 9–inch baking dish.

4   To begin preparations for the crust, place the eggs in a large bowl and beat them lightly. Place a saucepan over medium heat and melt the butter. Reduce the heat to medium-low and add the flour. Stir constantly until the mixture is smooth.

5   While stirring constantly, gradually add the milk and bring the mixture to a boil. When the mixture reaches a boil, remove the pan from heat. Stir approximately half of the mixture in the saucepan into the beaten eggs. Stir the tempered eggs into the saucepan and then add the cheese and dill or parsley. Stir to combine and pour the mixture over the lamb mixture in the baking dish, using a rubber spatula to smooth the top.

6   Place the baking dish in the oven and bake the moussaka until the crust is set and golden brown, about 35 minutes. Remove from the oven and let the moussaka rest for 5 minutes before serving.

INGREDIENTS

For the Filling

4 cups cold water

¼ cup kosher salt, plus more to taste

3 large eggplants, trimmed, cut into cubes

5 tablespoons extra-virgin olive oil

2 lbs. ground lamb

2 onions, diced

3 garlic cloves, minced

½ cup dry white wine

1 cup Marinara Sauce (see page 245)

2 tablespoons chopped fresh parsley

1 teaspoon dried oregano

½ teaspoon cinnamon

Black pepper, to taste

Freshly grated nutmeg, to taste

For the Crust

5 eggs

6 tablespoons unsalted butter

⅓ cup all-purpose flour

2½ cups milk

⅔ cup grated kefalotyri cheese

⅓ cup fresh dill or parsley, chopped

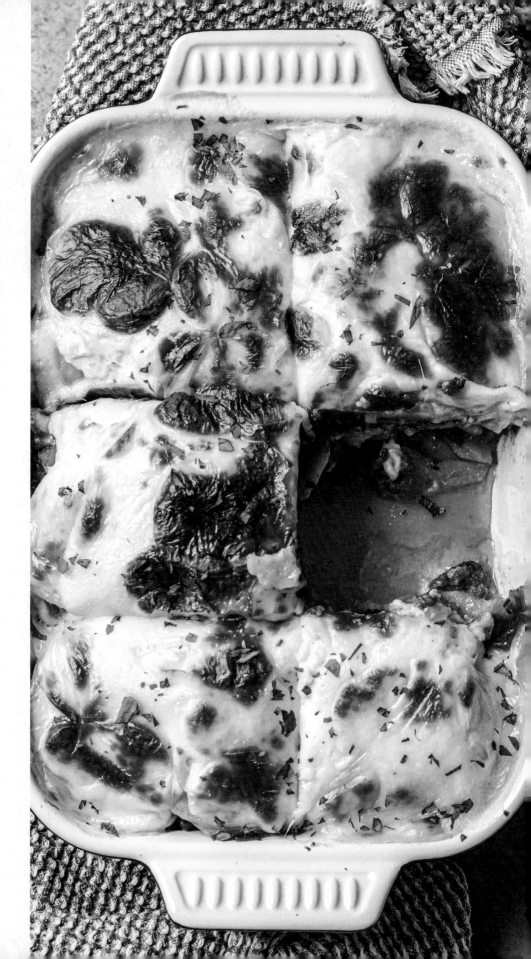

PORK WITH BLUE CHEESE POLENTA & ROASTED PEACH HOT SAUCE

YIELD: **6 SERVINGS** | ACTIVE TIME: **1 HOUR** | TOTAL TIME: **5 HOURS**

1   Preheat the oven to 300°F. Season the pork generously with salt, place it in a large skillet, and cook, turning as necessary, over medium-high heat until it is browned all over.

2   Transfer the pork shoulder to a Dutch oven and add the onion, bay leaves, paprika, brown sugar, peppercorns, 4 cups of the stock, and the mustard.

3   Cover the Dutch oven, place it in the oven, and cook until the pork is extremely tender, about 4 hours. Remove from the oven, let cool slightly, and then shred the pork shoulder with a fork.

4   Approximately 1 hour before the pulled pork will be finished cooking, place the cornmeal, the remaining stock, and the water in a large pot. Bring to a boil over medium-high heat, reduce the heat so that the mixture simmers, and cook, stirring continually for 2 minutes every 10 minutes or so, until the mixture is thick and creamy, about 40 minutes to 1 hour.

5   Stir half of the butter and half of the blue cheese into the polenta. Season it with salt and pepper, remove the pan from heat, and set it aside.

6   Once you have removed the pork shoulder from the oven, raise the oven's temperature to 400°F. Place the peaches on a baking sheet, cut side up, and place them in the oven. Roast until they began to darken, about 10 minutes. You can also grill the peaches if you're after a slightly smokier sauce.

7   Remove the peaches from the oven and place them in a medium saucepan. Add the vinegar, sugar, garlic, peppers, and lemon juice and bring to a simmer over medium-low heat. Simmer for 10 minutes, transfer the mixture to a blender, and puree until smooth. Set the hot sauce aside.

8   Stir the remaining butter into the polenta and then spoon the polenta into warmed bowls. Top each portion with some of the pulled pork, hot sauce, and remaining blue cheese.

INGREDIENTS

6- to 8-lb. bone-in pork shoulder

Salt and pepper, to taste

1 large yellow onion, chopped

3 bay leaves

2 teaspoons paprika

¼ cup brown sugar

2 tablespoons black peppercorns

7 cups Chicken Stock (see page 239)

1 tablespoon Dijon mustard

2 cups medium-grain cornmeal

2 cups water

½ cup unsalted butter

1 cup crumbled blue cheese

8 overly ripe peaches, pits removed, quartered

2 cups apple cider vinegar

¾ cup sugar

3 garlic cloves, chopped

6 jalapeño peppers, stems and seeds removed, diced

4 cayenne peppers, stems and seeds removed, diced

¼ cup fresh lemon juice

HEIRLOOM TOMATO & SMOKED CHEDDAR SOUP

YIELD: **6 SERVINGS** | ACTIVE TIME: **20 MINUTES** | TOTAL TIME: **1 HOUR AND 15 MINUTES**

INGREDIENTS

½ lb. unsalted butter

1 small red onion, sliced

3 celery stalks, sliced

10 garlic cloves, sliced

1 tablespoon kosher salt, plus more to taste

½ cup all-purpose flour

8 heirloom tomatoes, chopped

3 cups Marinara Sauce (see page 245)

1 tablespoon tomato paste

4 cups Vegetable Stock (see page 240)

1 Parmesan cheese rind (optional)

1 cup heavy cream

1 cup grated smoked cheddar cheese

10 fresh basil leaves, sliced thin

Black pepper, to taste

1. Place the butter in a large saucepan and melt it over medium heat. Add the onion, celery, garlic, and salt and cook, stirring frequently, until the onion is translucent, about 3 minutes.

2. Add the flour and cook, stirring continually, until it gives off a nutty aroma. Add the tomatoes, Marinara Sauce, tomato paste, stock, and, if using, the Parmesan rind. Stir to incorporate and let the soup come to a boil. Reduce the heat so that the soup simmers and cook for 30 minutes, stirring occasionally. Taste to see if the flavor has developed to your liking. If not, continue to simmer until it has.

3. Stir the cream, cheddar, and basil into the soup. Remove the Parmesan rind, transfer the soup to a blender, and puree until smooth. Season the soup with salt and pepper and ladle it into warmed bowls.

BUTTERNUT SQUASH & SAGE CANNELLONI

YIELD: **8 SERVINGS** | ACTIVE TIME: **1 HOUR** | TOTAL TIME: **1 HOUR AND 30 MINUTES**

INGREDIENTS

For the Filling

2 lbs. butternut squash, halved and seeded

5 tablespoons extra-virgin olive oil

5 garlic cloves, minced

1½ cups ricotta cheese

1 cup freshly grated Parmesan cheese

12 fresh sage leaves, sliced thin

1 teaspoon freshly grated nutmeg

Salt and white pepper, to taste

For the Cannelloni

1½ cups all-purpose flour, plus more as needed

1½ teaspoons kosher salt, plus more to taste

¾ cup egg yolks

1 tablespoon extra-virgin olive oil, plus more as needed

Semolina flour, as needed

1 To begin preparations for the filling, preheat the oven to 375°F. Brush the flesh of the squash with 1 tablespoon of the olive oil and place the squash on a parchment-lined baking sheet, cut side down. Place the baking sheet in the oven and roast until the squash is fork-tender, 40 to 45 minutes. Remove the squash from the oven and let it cool. When it is cool enough to handle, scoop the flesh into a wide, shallow bowl and mash it until smooth.

2 Warm a large skillet over low heat for 2 to 3 minutes. Add 2 tablespoons of the olive oil and the garlic and raise the heat to medium. Cook, stirring continually, for 1 minute, remove the pan from heat, and transfer the garlic and olive oil to the bowl with the pureed squash. Add the cheeses, half of the sage, and the nutmeg, season the mixture with salt and pepper, and stir to combine. Set the filling aside.

3 To begin preparations for the dough, place the all-purpose flour and salt in a mixing bowl, stir to combine, and make a well in the center. Pour the egg yolks and olive oil into the well and gradually incorporate the flour into the well. When all the flour has been incorporated, place the dough on a flour-dusted work surface and knead it until it is a smooth ball. Cover the dough with plastic wrap and let it rest at room temperature for 30 minutes.

4 Divide the dough into quarters. Use a rolling pin to flatten each quarter to a thickness that can go through the widest setting on a pasta maker. Roll the dough through a pasta maker until the sheets are about ⅟₁₆ inch thick. Lay the sheets on flour-dusted, parchment paper–lined baking sheets. Working with one sheet at a time, place it on a lightly floured work surface in front of you. Using a pastry cutter, cut each sheet into as many 4½- to 5-inch squares as possible. Place the finished squares on another lightly floured, parchment-lined baking sheet, making sure they don't touch. As you run out of room, lightly dust the squares with semolina flour, cover them with another sheet of parchment, and arrange more squares on top. Repeat with all the pasta sheets. Gather any scraps together into a ball, put It through the pasta machine to create additional pasta sheets, and cut those as well.

5 Bring a large pot of water to a boil. Once it's boiling, add salt and stir to dissolve. Add the squares and carefully stir for the first minute to prevent them from sticking. Cook until the pasta is just tender, about 2 minutes. Drain, rinse under cold water, and toss with a little bit of olive oil to keep them from sticking together.

6 Generously coat a baking dish—large enough to fit all the filled cannelloni in a single layer—with olive oil. To fill the cannelloni, place a pasta square in front of you. Place ¼ cup of the squash mixture in the center of the square and roll the pasta square around the filling into a tube. Place the cannelloni in the baking dish, seam side down. Repeat with the remaining sheets and filling. When the baking dish is filled, brush the tops of the cannelloni with olive oil.

7 Preheat the oven to 375°F and position a rack in the middle. Place the baking dish in the oven and bake the cannelloni until they are very hot and begin to turn golden brown, about 20 minutes.

8 Remove the cannelloni from the pan, top them with the remaining sage, and enjoy.

CHICKEN DE CHAMPIÑONES

YIELD: **4 SERVINGS** | ACTIVE TIME: **15 MINUTES** | TOTAL TIME: **15 MINUTES**

INGREDIENTS

2 tablespoons extra-virgin olive oil

1 lb. chicken cutlets

Salt and pepper, to taste

6 button mushrooms, quartered

1 shallot, chopped

1 garlic clove, sliced

¼ cup white wine

¼ cup heavy cream

¼ cup shredded Oaxaca cheese

1 teaspoon cumin

Fresh cilantro, chopped, for garnish

1   Place the olive oil in a skillet and warm it over medium-high heat. Season the chicken with salt and pepper, place it in the pan, and sear for 1 minute on each side.

2   Add the mushrooms and cook for about 30 seconds. Add the shallot and garlic and cook for another 30 seconds, stirring frequently.

3   Deglaze the pan with the white wine and cook until the liquid has reduced by half. Stir in the cream, Oaxaca cheese, and cumin and cook until the chicken is cooked through, about 6 minutes.

4   Garnish with the cilantro and enjoy.

CHICKEN BURRITOS

YIELD: **6 SERVINGS** | **ACTIVE TIME: 20 MINUTES** | **TOTAL TIME: 30 MINUTES**

INGREDIENTS

2 tablespoons extra-virgin olive oil

1 lb. boneless, skinless chicken breast

Salt and pepper, to taste

1 cup white rice

¼ cup chopped fresh cilantro

1 (14 oz.) can of black beans, drained and rinsed

1 small red onion, chopped

2 tomatoes, diced

1 cup grated pepper jack cheese

6 Flour Tortillas (see page 247)

Guacamole (see page 246), for serving

Pico de Gallo (see page 242), for serving

Sour cream, for serving

1   Place the olive oil in a large skillet and warm it over medium heat. Season the chicken with salt and pepper, place it in the pan, and cook, turning as necessary, until it is browned and cooked through, 8 to 10 minutes. Remove the chicken from the pan and let it rest for 10 minutes.

2   While the chicken is cooking and resting, prepare the rice according to the directions on the package.

3   Layer the rice, cilantro, beans, chicken, onion, tomatoes, and cheese on the tortillas. Roll them up tight and serve with Guacamole, Pico de Gallo, and sour cream.

BAKED EGG CASSEROLE

YIELD: **6 SERVINGS** | ACTIVE TIME: **15 MINUTES** | TOTAL TIME: **1 HOUR AND 10 MINUTES**

INGREDIENTS

12 large eggs

¼ cup water

½ cup half-and-half

3 plum tomatoes, sliced

1 cup chopped spinach

½ cup chopped scallions

1 cup freshly grated Parmesan cheese, plus more for garnish

1 tablespoon fresh thyme

1 tablespoon unsalted butter

Salt and pepper, to taste

1 Preheat the oven to 350°F. In a mixing bowl, combine the eggs, water, and half-and-half.

2 Place all of the other ingredients, except for the butter, salt, and pepper, in the mixing bowl and whisk to combine.

3 Coat a medium cast-iron skillet with the butter and then pour the mixture into the skillet.

4 Season the egg mixture with salt and pepper, place the skillet in the oven, and bake until the eggs are set in the center, about 45 minutes.

5 Remove the pan from the oven and let the casserole stand for 10 minutes before serving. Sprinkle additional Parmesan over the casserole and enjoy.

BUTTERNUT SQUASH RAVIOLI

YIELD: **6 SERVINGS** | ACTIVE TIME: **2 HOURS** | TOTAL TIME: **3 HOURS**

INGREDIENTS

1 cup "00" flour

Pinch of kosher salt, plus more to taste

10 egg yolks, beaten

1 teaspoon extra-virgin olive oil, plus more as needed

1½ lbs. butternut squash, halved lengthwise and seeded

1 tablespoon unsalted butter

¼ cup soft bread crumbs

½ cup grated Parmesan cheese, plus more for garnish

¼ cup crumbled gorgonzola cheese

1 teaspoon freshly grated nutmeg

10 fresh rosemary leaves, minced

1   Place the flour and salt in a mixing bowl, stir to combine, and make a well in the center. Place eight of the egg yolks and the olive oil in the well and slowly incorporate the flour until the dough holds together. Knead the dough until it is smooth, about 5 minutes. Cover the bowl with plastic wrap and let stand at room temperature for 30 minutes.

2   Preheat the oven to 375°F. Brush the flesh of the squash with olive oil and place it, cut side up, on a parchment-lined baking sheet. Place the squash in the oven and roast until it is fork-tender, 40 to 45 minutes. Remove the squash from the oven and let it cool, then scoop the flesh into a bowl and mash until it is smooth. Add the butter, bread crumbs, cheeses, remaining egg yolks, nutmeg, and rosemary to the squash and stir until thoroughly combined.

3   To begin forming the ravioli, divide the dough into two pieces. Use a pasta maker to roll each piece into a long, thin rectangle. Place one of the rectangles over a floured ravioli tray and place a teaspoon of the filling into each depression. Combine the beaten egg and water in a small bowl. Dip a pastry brush or a finger into the egg wash and lightly coat the edge of each ravioli with it. Gently lay the other rectangle over the piece in the ravioli tray. Use a ravioli rolling pin to gently cut out the ravioli. Remove the cut ravioli and place them on a flour-dusted baking sheet.

4   Bring a large saucepan of salted water to a boil. When the water is boiling, add the ravioli, stir to make sure they do not stick to the bottom, and cook until tender but still chewy, about 2 minutes. Drain, divide them between the serving plates, drizzle your preferred sauce over the top, and garnish with additional Parmesan.

BOLOGNAISE WITH PENNE

YIELD: **6 SERVINGS** | ACTIVE TIME: **45 MINUTES** | TOTAL TIME: **2 HOURS**

1   Place the olive oil and bacon in a cast-iron Dutch oven and cook the bacon over medium heat until it is crispy, 6 to 8 minutes. Add the beef, season the mixture with salt and pepper, and cook, breaking the beef up with a wooden spoon as it browns, until it is cooked through, about 8 minutes.

2   Remove the bacon and beef from the pot and set the mixture aside.

3   Add the carrot, celery, onion, and garlic to the Dutch oven, season the mixture with salt, and cook, stirring frequently, until the carrot is tender, about 8 minutes. Return the bacon and beef to the pan, stir in the thyme and sherry, and cook until the sherry has nearly evaporated.

4   Add the crushed tomatoes, reduce the heat to low, and cook the sauce for approximately 45 minutes, stirring often, until it has thickened to the desired consistency.

5   Stir the cream and sage into the sauce and gently simmer for another 15 minutes.

6   Bring water to a boil in a large saucepan. Add salt and the penne and cook until it is just shy of al dente, about 6 minutes. Reserve 1 cup of the pasta water, drain the penne, and then return it to the pan. Add the butter, sauce, and reserved pasta water and stir to combine. Add the Parmesan and stir until it has melted.

7   Garnish the dish with basil, red pepper flakes, and additional Parmesan.

INGREDIENTS

2 tablespoons extra-virgin olive oil

½ lb. bacon, chopped

1½ lbs. ground beef

Salt and pepper, to taste

1 carrot, peeled and minced

3 celery stalks, chopped

1 onion, chopped

2 garlic cloves, minced

1 tablespoon fresh thyme

2 cups sherry

8 cups crushed tomatoes

1 cup heavy cream

2 tablespoons finely chopped fresh sage

1 lb. penne

4 tablespoons unsalted butter

1 cup freshly grated Parmesan cheese, plus more for garnish

Fresh basil, for garnish

Red pepper flakes, for garnish

RISI E BISI

YIELD: **4 SERVINGS** | ACTIVE TIME: **30 MINUTES** | TOTAL TIME: **30 MINUTES**

INGREDIENTS

2 tablespoons extra-virgin olive oil

6 oz. thinly sliced prosciutto, cut into ¼-inch-wide strips

2 shallots, minced

1 garlic clove, minced

1 cup Arborio rice

½ cup white wine

Chicken Stock (see page 239), warmed, as needed

1 lb. frozen peas

1 cup freshly grated Parmesan cheese

Juice of ½ lemon

Salt and pepper, to taste

Fresh parsley, chopped, for garnish

1   Place the olive oil in a large cast-iron skillet and warm it over medium-high heat. Add the prosciutto and cook, stirring frequently, until it is golden brown and crispy, about 5 minutes. Using a slotted spoon, transfer the prosciutto to a paper towel–lined plate and let it drain.

2   Add the shallots to the skillet and cook, stirring occasionally, until they start to soften, about 3 minutes.

3   Add the garlic and rice and cook, stirring frequently, for 2 minutes.

4   Add the white wine and cook, stirring frequently, until the rice has absorbed the wine.

5   While stirring continually, add the stock ¼ cup at a time, waiting until each addition has been fully absorbed by the rice before adding more. Continue gradually adding stock until the rice is tender, about 15 minutes.

6   Add the frozen peas and cook, stirring frequently, until warmed through, 4 to 5 minutes.

7   Stir in the Parmesan and lemon juice. Season the dish with salt and pepper, garnish with the crispy prosciutto and parsley, and enjoy.

CAPRESE CHICKEN

YIELD: **6 SERVINGS** | ACTIVE TIME: **15 MINUTES** | TOTAL TIME: **45 MINUTES**

INGREDIENTS

1 garlic clove, minced

1 teaspoon dried oregano

1 teaspoon garlic powder

Salt and pepper, to taste

2 tablespoons extra-virgin
olive oil

2 lbs. boneless, skinless
chicken breasts, halved at
their equators

1 lb. tomatoes, sliced

1 lb. fresh mozzarella
cheese, drained and sliced

Leaves from 1 bunch of
fresh basil

Balsamic vinegar,
for garnish

1   Preheat the oven to 375°F. Place the garlic, oregano, garlic powder, salt, and pepper in a bowl and stir to combine. Place 1 tablespoon of the olive oil and the sliced chicken breasts in a bowl and toss to coat. Dredge the chicken breasts in the garlic-and-spice mixture until they are coated and set them aside.

2   Coat the bottom of a large cast-iron skillet with the remaining olive oil and warm it over medium-high heat. Working in batches, sear the chicken breasts for 1 minute on each side.

3   When all of the chicken has been seared, place half of the breasts in an even layer on the bottom of the skillet. Top with two-thirds of the tomatoes and mozzarella, and half of the basil leaves. Place the remaining chicken breasts on top in an even layer and cover this layer of chicken with the remaining tomatoes, mozzarella, and basil.

4   Place the skillet in the oven and cook until the interior temperature of the chicken breasts is 165°F, about 10 minutes.

5   Remove the skillet from the oven and let the chicken rest for 10 minutes. Drizzle the balsamic vinegar over the dish and enjoy.

SHRIMP & GRITS

YIELD: **6 SERVINGS** | ACTIVE TIME: **15 MINUTES** | TOTAL TIME: **1 HOUR AND 30 MINUTES**

INGREDIENTS

1 cup quick-cooking grits

2 large eggs

5 tablespoons unsalted butter, softened

¾ cup milk

Salt and pepper, to taste

1 lb. cheddar cheese, grated

1 tablespoon extra-virgin olive oil

1 lb. shrimp, shells removed, deveined

2 garlic cloves, minced

1 tablespoon fresh lemon juice

2 dashes of Tabasco

1   Preheat the oven to 425°F. Place 4 cups of water in a large cast-iron skillet and bring it to a boil. While stirring constantly, slowly pour in the grits. Cover the pan, reduce the heat to low, and cook, while stirring occasionally, until the grits are quite thick, about 5 minutes. Remove the pan from heat.

2   Place the eggs, 4 tablespoons of the butter, and the milk in a bowl, season the mixture with salt and pepper, and stir to combine. Stir the cooked grits into the egg mixture, add three-quarters of the cheese, and stir to incorporate.

3   Wipe out the skillet, coat it with the remaining butter, and pour the grits mixture into the skillet. Place the skillet in the oven and bake for 30 minutes. Remove, sprinkle the remaining cheese on top, and return the grits to the oven. Bake until the cheese is melted and the grits are firm, about 15 minutes. Remove the grits from the oven and let them cool for 10 minutes.

4   Place the olive oil in a medium cast-iron skillet and warm it over medium-high heat. Add the shrimp to the skillet, season them with salt and pepper, and cook for 1 minute. Turn the shrimp over, stir in the garlic, lemon juice, and Tabasco, and cook until the shrimp are pink and opaque throughout, 1 to 2 minutes.

5   Divide the grits among four bowls, place a few shrimp on top of each portion, and enjoy.

SKILLET LASAGNA

YIELD: **6 SERVINGS** | ACTIVE TIME: **30 MINUTES** | TOTAL TIME: **45 MINUTES**

INGREDIENTS

2 tablespoons extra-virgin olive oil

1 onion, sliced thin

4 garlic cloves, sliced thin

2 zucchini, chopped

1 cup chopped eggplant

2 cups baby spinach

1 (28 oz.) can of whole peeled San Marzano tomatoes, with their liquid, crushed by hand

Salt and pepper, to taste

8 no-cook lasagna noodles

1 cup ricotta cheese

½ cup freshly grated Parmesan cheese, plus more for garnish

½ lb. fresh mozzarella cheese, sliced thin

Fresh basil, finely chopped, for garnish

1 Place the olive oil in a large cast-iron skillet and warm it over medium-low heat. Add the onion and cook, stirring occasionally, until it has softened, about 5 minutes.

2 Add the garlic and cook, stirring continually, for 1 minute. Raise the heat to medium, add the zucchini and eggplant, and cook, stirring occasionally, until the zucchini has softened and the eggplant has collapsed, about 10 minutes.

3 Add the spinach and cook, stirring continually, until it has wilted, about 2 minutes. Transfer the vegetable mixture to a bowl.

4 Cover the bottom of the skillet with a thin layer of the tomatoes and season with salt and pepper. Top with 4 lasagna noodles, breaking off the edges as necessary to fit the pan. Spread half of the vegetable mixture over the noodles and dot the mixture with dollops of ricotta. Top with one-third of the remaining tomatoes, season them with salt and pepper, and spread the remaining vegetable mixture over the top. Dot the vegetables with dollops of the remaining ricotta. Top with the remaining lasagna noodles, spread the remaining tomatoes over the top, and then layer the Parmesan and mozzarella over the tomatoes.

5 Season with salt and pepper, cover the skillet, and cook over medium-low heat until the pasta is soft and the cheese has completely melted, 5 to 10 minutes.

6 Uncover the skillet, raise the heat to medium-high, and cook until the sauce has thickened, about 5 minutes. Remove the pan from heat and let the lasagna cool slightly, 5 to 10 minutes, before cutting. Sprinkle the basil over the lasagna and enjoy.

SPINACH STRATA

YIELD: **8 SERVINGS** | ACTIVE TIME: **20 MINUTES** | TOTAL TIME: **1 HOUR**

INGREDIENTS

7 eggs, beaten

2 cups whole milk

1 cup shredded Swiss cheese

Pinch of freshly grated nutmeg

3 cups day-old bread pieces

2 teaspoons extra-virgin olive oil

1 yellow onion, minced

5 oz. baby spinach

Salt and pepper, to taste

1 Preheat the oven to 400°F. Place the eggs and milk in a large mixing bowl and whisk to combine. Add the cheese and nutmeg and stir to incorporate. Add the bread pieces and let the mixture sit for 10 minutes.

2 Place the olive oil in a 10-inch cast-iron skillet and warm it over medium heat. Add the onion and spinach and cook, stirring occasionally, until the spinach has wilted and the onion is translucent, about 3 minutes. Remove the pan from heat.

3 Pour the egg mixture into the skillet and gently shake the pan to make sure the eggs are evenly distributed. Season the strata with salt and pepper.

4 Place the skillet in the oven and bake the strata until it is golden brown and springy in the center, about 25 minutes.

5 Remove the strata from the oven and let it cool for 10 minutes before enjoying.

EGGPLANT PARMESAN

YIELD: **4 SERVINGS** | ACTIVE TIME: **20 MINUTES** | TOTAL TIME: **1 HOUR AND 15 MINUTES**

INGREDIENTS

1 large eggplant

Salt, to taste

2 tablespoons extra-virgin olive oil

1 cup Italian bread crumbs

¼ cup freshly grated Parmesan cheese

1 egg, beaten

Marinara Sauce (see page 245), as needed

2 garlic cloves, minced

½ lb. shredded mozzarella cheese

Fresh basil, finely chopped, for garnish

1   Preheat the oven to 350°F. Trim the top and bottom off the eggplant and cut it into ¼-inch-thick slices. Put the slices on paper towels in a single layer, sprinkle salt over them, and let them rest for about 15 minutes. Turn the slices over, salt the other side, and let them rest for another 15 minutes. Rinse the eggplant and pat it dry with paper towels.

2   Drizzle the olive oil over a baking sheet. In a shallow bowl, combine the bread crumbs and Parmesan cheese. Put the beaten egg in another shallow bowl. Dredge the slices of eggplant in the egg and then in the bread crumb-and-cheese mixture until both sides are completely coated. Place the breaded eggplant on the baking sheet.

3   When all of the eggplant has been breaded, place it in the oven and bake for 10 minutes. Remove the pan from the oven, turn the slices of eggplant over, and bake until the eggplant is golden brown, about 10 minutes. Remove the eggplant from the oven and let it cool slightly.

4   Place a layer of sauce in a square 8-inch baking dish or a cast-iron skillet and stir in the garlic. Lay some of the eggplant slices on top of the sauce, top them with more sauce, and then arrange the remaining eggplant on top. Sprinkle the mozzarella over the eggplant.

5   Place the dish in the oven and bake for about 30 minutes, until the sauce is bubbling and the cheese is golden brown. Remove from the oven and let cool for 10 minutes before serving with additional Marinara Sauce and fresh basil.

SQUASH BLOSSOM & RICOTTA PIZZA

YIELD: **1 PIZZA** | ACTIVE TIME: **15 MINUTES** | TOTAL TIME: **45 MINUTES**

INGREDIENTS

Semolina flour, as needed

1 ball of pizza dough

Extra-virgin olive oil, to taste

4 oz. low-moisture mozzarella cheese, shredded

3 squash blossoms, stamens removed, sliced lengthwise

3 oz. ricotta cheese

Salt and pepper, to taste

Zest of 1 lemon

1 Preheat the oven to the maximum temperature and place a baking stone or steel on the bottom of the oven as it warms. Dust a work surface with semolina flour, place the dough on the surface, and gently stretch it into a round.

2 Drizzle olive oil over the dough, cover it with the shredded mozzarella, and distribute the squash blossoms over the cheese. You want to open the squash blossoms up so that they cover as much of the pizza as possible. Distribute dollops of the ricotta over the pizza, season with salt and pepper, and drizzle more olive oil over the top.

3 Dust a peel or a flat baking sheet with semolina and use it to transfer the pizza to the heated baking implement in the oven. Bake for 15 minutes, until the crust is golden brown and starting to char. Remove, sprinkle the lemon zest over the pizza, and let it cool slightly before serving.

POTATO & PESTO PIZZA

YIELD: **1 PIZZA** | ACTIVE TIME: **20 MINUTES** | TOTAL TIME: **1 HOUR**

INGREDIENTS

Salt and pepper, to taste

1 small potato, sliced

Semolina flour, as needed

1 ball of pizza dough

3 oz. caciocavallo
cheese, sliced

2 tablespoons Pesto (see
page 66)

Extra-virgin olive oil,
as needed

1   Preheat the oven to the maximum temperature and place a baking stone or steel on the bottom of the oven as it warms. Bring salted water to a boil in a saucepan and prepare an ice water bath. Add the potato to the boiling water, cook until it is translucent, 2 to 4 minutes, drain, and place it in the ice water bath. Let the potato sit for 2 minutes, drain, and pat dry with paper towels.

2   Dust a work surface with semolina flour, place the dough on the surface, and gently stretch it into a round. Distribute the cheese, potato, and pesto over the dough, drizzle olive oil over everything, and season the pizza with salt and pepper.

3   Dust a peel or a flat baking sheet with semolina and use it to transfer the pizza to the heated baking implement in the oven. Bake for about 15 minutes, until the crust is golden brown and starting to char. Remove and let cool slightly before slicing and serving.

PIZZA WITH ZUCCHINI CREAM, BACON & BUFFALO MOZZARELLA

YIELD: **1 PIZZA** | ACTIVE TIME: **15 MINUTES** | TOTAL TIME: **45 MINUTES**

INGREDIENTS

Semolina flour, as needed

1 ball of pizza dough

3 tablespoons Zucchini Cream (see page 236)

3½ oz. buffalo mozzarella cheese, drained and chopped

Extra-virgin olive oil, to taste

2 slices of bacon, cooked and crumbled

1   Preheat the oven to the maximum temperature and place a baking stone or steel on the bottom of the oven as it warms. Dust a work surface with the semolina flour, place the dough on the surface, and gently stretch it into a round.

2   Cover the dough with the Zucchini Cream, distribute the mozzarella over it, and drizzle olive oil over the top.

3   Dust a peel or a flat baking sheet with semolina and use it to transfer the pizza to the heated baking implement in the oven. Bake for about 15 minutes, until the crust is golden brown and starting to char. Remove and let cool slightly before sprinkling the bacon over the pizza, slicing, and serving.

CHILAQUILES

YIELD: **4 SERVINGS** | ACTIVE TIME: **30 MINUTES** | TOTAL TIME: **45 MINUTES**

INGREDIENTS

½ lb. tomatillos, husked and rinsed well

2 garlic cloves

½ red onion, sliced thin

2 guajillo chile peppers, stems and seeds removed

2 dried chiles de árbol, stems and seeds removed

2 cups canola oil

1 lb. Corn Tortillas (see page 243), cut into 40 triangles

Salt, to taste

2 tablespoons extra-virgin olive oil

4 large eggs

2 cups crumbled queso fresco, plus more for serving

Fresh cilantro, chopped, for garnish

Sour cream, for serving

Lime wedges, for serving

1 Bring water to a boil in a medium saucepan. Add the tomatillos, garlic, and half of the onion and cook until it is tender, about 7 minutes.

2 While the vegetables are boiling, place the chiles in a bowl and pour some hot water over them. Let the chiles soak for 15 minutes.

3 Drain the vegetables, place them in a blender, and puree until smooth. Leave the puree in the blender.

4 Place the canola oil in a large, deep cast-iron skillet and warm it to 350°F. Add the tortillas and fry until crispy, about 3 minutes. Place the fried tortillas on a paper towel–lined plate and let them drain. Wipe out the skillet.

5 Preheat the oven to 350°F. Add the chiles to the puree in the blender and puree until smooth. Season the puree generously with salt and set it aside.

6 Place the olive oil in the skillet and warm it over medium heat. Add the remaining onion and cook, stirring occasionally, until it is translucent, about 3 minutes.

7 Add the puree and the tortillas to the skillet and stir until everything is combined. Crack the eggs on top, crumble the queso fresco over everything, and place the skillet in the oven.

8 Bake until the egg whites are set and the cheese is slightly melted. Remove the skillet from the oven and garnish the chilaquiles with cilantro. Serve with sour cream, additional queso fresco, and lime wedges.

FETTUCCINE ALFREDO

YIELD: **4 SERVINGS** | ACTIVE TIME: **15 MINUTES** | TOTAL TIME: **15 MINUTES**

INGREDIENTS

Salt and pepper, to taste

¾ lb. fettuccine

½ cup heavy cream

2½ tablespoons
unsalted butter, at room
temperature

1 cup grated Parmesan
cheese, plus more
for garnish

½ teaspoon freshly grated
nutmeg

1   Bring a large pot of water to a boil. Once it's boiling, add salt to taste and the fettuccine and cook for 6 minutes. Reserve ½ cup of pasta water and drain the fettuccine.

2   Place the reserved pasta water and heavy cream in a large skillet and bring it to a simmer. Add the butter and stir until it has been emulsified. Gradually incorporate the Parmesan, making sure each addition has melted before adding the next.

3   Add the fettuccine to the skillet and toss to combine. Sprinkle the nutmeg and additional Parmesan over the top and season with pepper before serving.

SHAKSHUKA

YIELD: **4 SERVINGS** | ACTIVE TIME: **30 MINUTES** | TOTAL TIME: **1 HOUR**

INGREDIENTS

2 tablespoons extra-virgin olive oil

1 onion, chopped

2 green bell peppers, stems and seeds removed, chopped

2 garlic cloves, minced

1 teaspoon coriander

1 teaspoon sweet paprika

½ teaspoon cumin

1 teaspoon turmeric

Pinch of red pepper flakes

2 tablespoons tomato paste

5 ripe tomatoes, chopped

Salt and pepper, to taste

6 eggs

1 cup crumbled feta cheese

¼ cup chopped fresh parsley, for garnish

¼ cup chopped fresh mint, for garnish

1   Place the olive oil in a large cast-iron skillet and warm it over medium heat. Add the onion and cook, stirring occasionally, until it has softened, about 5 minutes. Add the bell peppers and cook, stirring occasionally, until they have softened, about 5 minutes.

2   Add the garlic, coriander, paprika, cumin, turmeric, red pepper flakes, and tomato paste and cook, stirring continually, for 1 minute. Add the tomatoes and bring the mixture to a boil. Reduce the heat, cover the pan, and simmer for 15 minutes.

3   Remove the cover and cook until the shakshuka has reduced slightly, about 5 minutes.

4   Season the shakshuka with salt and pepper. Using the back of a wooden spoon, make six wells in the mixture. Crack an egg into each well and sprinkle the feta over the shakshuka.

5   Reduce the heat to a simmer, cover the pan, and cook until the egg whites are set, 6 to 8 minutes.

6   Remove the pan from heat, garnish with the parsley and mint, and enjoy.

BAKED ORZO

YIELD: **4 TO 6 SERVINGS** | ACTIVE TIME: **30 MINUTES** | TOTAL TIME: **1 HOUR AND 30 MINUTES**

INGREDIENTS

2 cups orzo

3 tablespoons extra-virgin olive oil

1 eggplant, seeds removed, chopped into ½-inch cubes

1 onion, chopped

4 garlic cloves, minced

2 teaspoons dried oregano

1 tablespoon tomato paste

3 cups Chicken Stock (see page 239)

1 cup freshly grated Parmesan cheese

2 tablespoons capers, drained and chopped

Salt and pepper, to taste

2 tomatoes, sliced thin

2 zucchini, sliced thin

1 cup crumbled feta cheese

1   Preheat the oven to 350°F. Place the orzo in a medium saucepan and toast it, stirring frequently, over medium heat until it is lightly browned, about 10 minutes. Transfer the orzo to a bowl.

2   Place 2 tablespoons of the olive oil in the saucepan and warm it over medium heat. Add the eggplant and cook, stirring occasionally, until it has browned, about 10 minutes. Remove the eggplant from the pan and place it in the bowl with the orzo.

3   Add the remaining olive oil to the saucepan and warm it over medium heat. Add the onion and cook, stirring occasionally, until it has softened, about 5 minutes. Add the garlic, oregano, and tomato paste and cook, stirring continually, for 1 minute.

4   Remove the pan from heat, add the stock, Parmesan, capers, orzo, and eggplant, season the mixture with salt and pepper, and stir to combine. Pour the mixture into a 10 x 8–inch baking dish.

5   Alternating rows, layer the tomatoes and zucchini on top of the orzo mixture. Season with salt and pepper.

6   Place the baking dish in the oven and bake until the orzo is tender, about 30 minutes.

7   Remove the dish from the oven, sprinkle the feta on top, and enjoy.

LOBSTER & CORN SALAD

YIELD: **4 SERVINGS** | ACTIVE TIME: **25 MINUTES** | TOTAL TIME: **50 MINUTES**

INGREDIENTS

For the Salad

¼ cup mayonnaise

¼ cup crema or sour cream

1 teaspoon fresh lime juice

¼ teaspoon Tapatío hot sauce

½ cup grated queso enchilado

Salt and pepper, to taste

Kernels from 2 ears of corn

2 tablespoons unsalted butter, melted

For the Lobster

½ cup unsalted butter

6 oz. lobster tail

2 tablespoons Tajín

Fresh cilantro, finely chopped, for garnish

1   To begin preparations for the salad, preheat the oven to 375°F. Place the mayonnaise, crema, lime juice, Tapatío, queso enchilado, salt, and pepper in a salad bowl, stir to combine, and set the mixture aside.

2   Place the corn kernels in small mixing bowl, along with the butter, and toss to combine. Place the corn kernels in an even layer on a baking sheet, place them in the oven, and roast until the corn is golden brown, 15 to 20 minutes.

3   Stir the corn into the salad bowl and let it cool. Chill the salad in the refrigerator.

4   To begin preparations for the lobster, place the butter in a skillet and warm over medium-low heat.

5   Remove the meat from the lobster tail using kitchen scissors. Add the meat to the pan and poach until it turns a reddish orange, 4 to 5 minutes. Remove the lobster meat from the pan with a slotted spoon and let it cool.

6   Slice the lobster into small medallions. To serve, spoon the corn salad onto each plate and arrange a few lobster medallions on top of each portion. Sprinkle the Tajín over the dishes and garnish with cilantro.

PASTA PRIMAVERA

YIELD: **4 TO 6 SERVINGS** | ACTIVE TIME: **15 MINUTES** | TOTAL TIME: **15 MINUTES**

INGREDIENTS

2 tablespoons unsalted butter

1 cup peas

½ lb. asparagus, trimmed and chopped

3 scallions, trimmed and chopped

2 garlic cloves, minced

Salt and pepper, to taste

¾ lb. fettuccine

½ cup full-fat Greek yogurt

⅔ cup grated Parmesan cheese, plus more for garnish

3 tablespoons chopped fresh parsley, for garnish

2 tablespoons chopped fresh tarragon, for garnish

1   Bring water to a boil in a large saucepan. Place the butter in a large skillet and melt it over medium heat. Add the peas, asparagus, scallions, and garlic, season it with salt and pepper, and cook, stirring constantly, until the asparagus is tender, about 4 minutes. Transfer the mixture to a bowl.

2   Place the pasta in the water and cook until it is al dente, about 6 minutes. Drain the pasta and add it to the vegetable mixture.

3   Add the yogurt and Parmesan and toss to combine. Garnish the dish with the parsley and tarragon and enjoy.

CHICKEN PANINI WITH SUN-DRIED TOMATO AIOLI

YIELD: **4 SERVINGS** | ACTIVE TIME: **10 MINUTES** | TOTAL TIME: **10 MINUTES**

INGREDIENTS

For the Aioli

1 cup sun-dried tomatoes in olive oil, drained and chopped

1 cup mayonnaise

1 tablespoon whole grain mustard

2 tablespoons finely chopped fresh parsley

2 tablespoons minced scallions

1 teaspoon white balsamic vinegar

1 garlic clove, minced

2 teaspoons kosher salt

1 teaspoon black pepper

For the Sandwiches

8 slices of crusty bread

8 slices of cheddar cheese

2 leftover chicken breasts, sliced

12 slices of cooked bacon

1 cup arugula

1. Preheat a panini press. To prepare the aioli, place all of the ingredients in a mixing bowl and stir until combined.

2. To begin preparations for the sandwiches, spread some of the aioli on each slice of bread. Place a slice of cheddar on each slice of bread. Divide the chicken between four pieces of the bread. Top each portion of chicken with 3 slices of bacon and ¼ cup of the arugula and assemble the sandwiches.

3. Place the sandwiches in the panini press and press until the cheese has melted and there is a nice crust on the bread. Remove and serve immediately.

Note: If you don't have a panini press, don't worry. Simply place 1 tablespoon of olive oil in a large skillet and warm over medium-high heat. Place a sandwich in the pan, place a warmed cast-iron skillet on top so it is pressing down on the sandwich, and cook until golden brown. Turn the sandwich over and repeat.

SPRING RISOTTO

YIELD: **4 SERVINGS** | ACTIVE TIME: **45 MINUTES** | TOTAL TIME: **1 HOUR**

INGREDIENTS

½ cup chopped fresh chives

½ cup plus 2 tablespoons extra-virgin olive oil

½ teaspoon kosher salt, plus more to taste

½ lb. asparagus, trimmed

2 cups Vegetable Stock (see page 240)

1 tablespoon unsalted butter

2 tablespoons chopped shallot

½ cup minced fennel

1 cup Arborio rice

¼ cup dry white wine

¼ cup grated Fontina cheese, plus more for garnish

Black pepper, to taste

1 tablespoon fresh lemon juice

4 oz. mushrooms, separated and trimmed

1. Preheat the oven to 400°F. Place the chives, the ½ cup of olive oil, and the salt in a blender and puree until smooth. Set the mixture aside.

2. Place the asparagus on a baking sheet, place it in the oven, and roast until it is tender, 15 to 20 minutes. Remove the asparagus from the oven and briefly let it cool. Chop the asparagus into 1-inch pieces and set it aside.

3. Place the stock in a small saucepan and bring it to a simmer over medium heat. Turn off the heat and leave the pan on the stove. Place the butter and 1 tablespoon of the remaining olive oil in a large skillet and warm the mixture over medium heat. Add the shallot and fennel and cook, stirring frequently, until they just start to brown, about 5 minutes. Add the rice and toast it until it starts to give off a nutty aroma, stirring continually.

4. Deglaze the pan with the white wine, scraping up any browned bits from the bottom of the pan. When the wine has been fully absorbed by the rice, add the warm stock a little at a time, stirring constantly to prevent sticking, and cook until the rice absorbs it. If the rice is still crunchy by the time you have used up all of the stock, incorporate water in 1-tablespoon increments until it reaches the desired tenderness.

5. When the rice is a few minutes from being done—still a little too firm—stir in the asparagus. When the rice is al dente, stir in the cheese, season with salt and pepper, and add the lemon juice. Stir to incorporate and turn off the heat.

6. Place the remaining olive oil in a large skillet, warm it over medium-high heat, and then add the mushrooms in a single layer. Add a pinch of salt and cook until the mushrooms start to brown, about 5 minutes. Turn the mushrooms over, add another pinch of salt, and cook for another 5 minutes.

7. Divide the risotto between four warmed bowls and top each portion with a few mushrooms. Drizzle the chive-infused oil over the top and sprinkle additional Fontina on top.

HAM & SWISS QUICHE

YIELD: **1 QUICHE** | ACTIVE TIME: **15 MINUTES** | TOTAL TIME: **2 HOURS**

INGREDIENTS

8 eggs

1 cup heavy cream

1 teaspoon kosher salt

¼ teaspoon black pepper

8 slices of Swiss cheese

1 Perfect Piecrust (see page 248), blind baked

8 slices of smoked ham

1   Preheat the oven to 350°F. Place the eggs, heavy cream, salt, and pepper in a mixing bowl and whisk until combined. Set the mixture aside.

2   Lay two slices of the cheese on the bottom of the crust, followed by two slices of the ham. Alternate layers of cheese and ham until all of the slices have been used.

3   Pour the egg mixture into the crust, stopping when it reaches the top.

4   Place the quiche in the oven and bake until the center is set and the filling is lightly golden brown, 35 to 45 minutes.

5   Remove the quiche from the oven, transfer it to a wire rack, and let it cool for 1 hour before serving. The quiche will be enjoyable warm, at room temperature, or cold.

GRILLED CHEESE

YIELD: **2 SERVINGS** | ACTIVE TIME: **10 MINUTES** | TOTAL TIME: **10 MINUTES**

INGREDIENTS

2 oz. cheddar cheese, grated

2 oz. Gruyère cheese, grated

4 slices of bread (½ inch thick)

2 tablespoons unsalted butter

1   Place the cheeses in a bowl and stir to combine.

2   Divide the cheese mixture between two slices of the bread. Top with the remaining slices of bread and press down gently.

3   Place 1 tablespoon of the butter in a large skillet and melt it over medium heat. Add the sandwiches to the pan and cook until the bottoms turn golden brown, 3 to 4 minutes, reducing the heat if necessary to keep the toast from burning.

4   Add the remaining butter, flip the sandwiches over, press down on them, and cook until the cheese is completely melted and both sides of the sandwich are golden brown, about 4 minutes. Enjoy immediately.

SPAGHETTI ALLA CARBONARA

YIELD: **4 SERVINGS** | ACTIVE TIME: **15 MINUTES** | TOTAL TIME: **15 MINUTES**

INGREDIENTS

2½ tablespoons extra-virgin olive oil

4 oz. pancetta or bacon, diced

Salt and pepper, to taste

2 large eggs, at room temperature

¾ cup freshly grated Parmesan cheese, plus more for garnish

1 lb. spaghetti

1   Bring a large saucepan of water to a boil. Add 2 tablespoons of the olive oil to a large skillet and warm it over medium heat. When the oil starts to shimmer, add the pancetta or bacon, and season it with pepper. Sauté the pancetta or bacon until its fat renders and the meat starts turning golden brown, about 5 minutes. Remove the skillet from heat and cover it partially.

2   Place the eggs in a small bowl and whisk until scrambled. Add the Parmesan, season with salt and pepper, and stir until combined.

3   Add salt and the pasta to the boiling water. Cook 2 minutes short of the directed cooking time, reserve ¼ cup of the pasta water, and drain the pasta.

4   Return the pot to the stove, raise the heat to high, and add the remaining olive oil and the reserved pasta water. Add the drained pasta and toss to combine. Cook until the pasta has absorbed the water.

5   Remove the pot from heat, add the pancetta or bacon and the egg-and-Parmesan mixture, and toss to coat the pasta. Divide the pasta between the serving bowls, season with pepper, and top each portion with additional Parmesan.

STUFFED PEPPERS, MEDITERRANEAN STYLE

YIELD: **4 SERVINGS** | ACTIVE TIME: **15 MINUTES** | TOTAL TIME: **15 MINUTES**

INGREDIENTS

4 yellow bell peppers, seeds removed, halved

12 cherry tomatoes, halved

2 garlic cloves, minced

2 tablespoons extra-virgin olive oil

½ cup crumbled feta cheese

1 cup black olives, pits removed

Salt and pepper, to taste

Leaves from 1 bunch of fresh basil

1 Preheat the oven to 375°F and place the peppers on a parchment-lined baking sheet.

2 Place the cherry tomatoes, garlic, olive oil, feta, and black olives in a mixing bowl and stir to combine. Divide the mixture between the peppers, place them in the oven, and roast until the peppers start to collapse, about 10 minutes.

3 Remove the peppers from the oven, season them with salt and pepper, top with the basil leaves, and enjoy.

DESSERTS

Between the affection fostered by the classic cheesecake and the cannoli, everyone is familiar with cheese's ability to bring a great meal to a fitting conclusion. But, when you stop and recognize that cheese is even capable of elevating the carrot to the decadent level required of a dessert, its full potential becomes apparent. These aforementioned classics can be found inside, along with a few innovative preparations that will send your appetite for cheese-based confections into overdrive.

RED VELVET CAKE

YIELD: **1 CAKE** | ACTIVE TIME: **1 HOUR** | TOTAL TIME: **3 HOURS**

INGREDIENTS

12.7 oz. cake flour

1 oz. cocoa powder

½ teaspoon kosher salt

1 teaspoon baking soda

13.4 oz. unsalted butter, softened

14½ oz. sugar

6 eggs

1 teaspoon white vinegar

2½ oz. buttermilk

1 teaspoon pure vanilla extract

2 teaspoons red food coloring

Cream Cheese Frosting (see page 193)

1 Preheat the oven to 350°F. Line three round 8-inch cake pans with parchment paper and coat them with nonstick cooking spray.

2 In a medium bowl, whisk together the cake flour, cocoa powder, salt, and baking soda. Set the mixture aside.

3 In the work bowl of a stand mixer fitted with the paddle attachment, cream the butter and sugar on high until the mixture is creamy and fluffy, about 5 minutes. Reduce the speed to low, add the eggs two at a time, and beat until incorporated, scraping down the side of the work bowl with a rubber spatula between additions. Add the vinegar, beat until incorporated, and then add the dry mixture. Beat until thoroughly incorporated, add the buttermilk, vanilla, and food coloring, and beat until they have been incorporated.

4 Pour 1½ cups of batter into each cake pan. Tap the pans on the counter to distribute the batter evenly and remove any air bubbles.

5 Place the cakes in the oven and bake until set and cooked through and a cake tester comes out clean after being inserted, 26 to 28 minutes. Remove the cakes from the oven, transfer them to a cooling rack, and let them cool completely.

6 Trim a thin layer off the top of each cake to create a flat surface. Transfer 2 cups of the frosting into a piping bag.

7 Place one cake on a cake stand and place 1 cup of the frosting in the center and level it with an offset spatula. Place the second cake on top and repeat the process with the frosting. Place the last cake on top and spread the remaining frosting over the entire cake, using an offset spatula. Refrigerate the cake for at least 1 hour before slicing and serving.

CREAM CHEESE FROSTING

YIELD: **3 CUPS** | ACTIVE TIME: **10 MINUTES** | TOTAL TIME: **10 MINUTES**

INGREDIENTS

1 cup unsalted butter, softened

½ lb. cream cheese, softened

2 lbs. confectioners' sugar

⅛ teaspoon kosher salt

¼ cup heavy cream

½ teaspoon pure vanilla extract

1 In the work bowl of a stand mixer fitted with the paddle attachment, combine the butter, cream cheese, confectioners' sugar, and salt and beat on low until the sugar starts to be incorporated into the butter. Raise the speed to high and beat until the mixture is smooth and fluffy, about 5 minutes.

2 Reduce the speed to low, add the heavy cream and vanilla, and beat until incorporated. Use immediately, or store in the refrigerator for up to 2 weeks. If refrigerating, return to room temperature before using.

CARROT CAKE

YIELD: **1 CAKE** | ACTIVE TIME: **20 MINUTES** | TOTAL TIME: **2 HOURS AND 15 MINUTES**

INGREDIENTS

2 cups shredded carrots, plus more for topping

2 cups sugar

1½ cups all-purpose flour

1½ tablespoons baking soda

1 teaspoon fine sea salt

1 tablespoon cinnamon

3 eggs

1¾ cups extra-virgin olive oil

2 teaspoons pure vanilla extract

½ cup chopped walnuts (optional)

Cream Cheese Frosting (see page 193)

1 Preheat the oven to 350°F. Place the carrots and sugar in a mixing bowl, stir to combine, and let the mixture sit for 10 minutes.

2 Place the flour, baking soda, salt, and cinnamon in a mixing bowl and stir to combine. Place the eggs, olive oil, and vanilla in a separate mixing bowl and stir to combine. Add the wet mixture to the dry mixture and stir until it comes together as a smooth batter. Stir in the carrots and walnuts (if desired).

3 Coat a 9-inch cake pan with butter, transfer the batter to the pan, and place the pan in the oven.

4 Bake the cake until it is golden brown and a toothpick inserted into the center comes out clean, 40 to 50 minutes.

5 Remove the cake from the oven, transfer it to a wire rack, and let it cool for 1 hour.

6 Spread the frosting over the cake, top it with additional shredded carrots, and enjoy.

CHEESECAKE WITH CITRUS & BRIE

YIELD: **1 CHEESECAKE** | ACTIVE TIME: **1 HOUR** | TOTAL TIME: **8 HOURS**

INGREDIENTS

1½ lbs. cream cheese, softened

½ lb. triple-cream Brie cheese, rind removed

⅔ cup sugar

¼ teaspoon kosher salt

Zest of 1 orange

4 eggs

1 tablespoon pure vanilla extract

2 tablespoons Grand Marnier

1 Graham Cracker Crust (see page 249), in a springform pan

1 Preheat the oven to 350°F. Bring 8 cups of water to a boil in a small saucepan.

2 In the work bowl of a stand mixer fitted with the paddle attachment, cream the cream cheese, Brie, sugar, salt, and orange zest on high until the mixture is fluffy, about 10 minutes. Scrape down the sides of the work bowl as needed.

3 Reduce the speed of the mixer to medium and incorporate one egg at a time, scraping down the work bowl as needed. Add the vanilla and Grand Marnier and mix until incorporated.

4 Pour the mixture into the crust, place the cheesecake in a large baking pan with high sides, and gently pour the boiling water into the baking pan until it reaches halfway up the sides of the springform pan.

5 Cover the baking pan with aluminum foil, place it in the oven, and bake until the cheesecake is set and only slightly jiggly in the center, 50 minutes to 1 hour.

6 Turn off the oven and leave the oven door cracked. Allow the cheesecake to sit in the cooling oven for 45 minutes.

7 Remove the cheesecake from the oven and transfer it to a cooling rack. Let it sit at room temperature for 1 hour.

8 Transfer the cheesecake to the refrigerator and let it cool for at least 4 hours before serving and slicing.

CLASSIC CHEESECAKE

YIELD: **1 CHEESECAKE** | ACTIVE TIME: **1 HOUR** | TOTAL TIME: **8 HOURS**

INGREDIENTS

2 lbs. cream cheese, softened

⅔ cup sugar

¼ teaspoon kosher salt

4 eggs

1 tablespoon pure vanilla extract

1 Graham Cracker Crust (see page 249), in a springform pan

1 Preheat the oven to 350°F. Bring 8 cups of water to a boil in a small saucepan.

2 In the work bowl of a stand mixer fitted with the paddle attachment, cream the cream cheese, sugar, and salt on high until the mixture is fluffy, about 10 minutes. Scrape down the side of the work bowl as needed.

3 Reduce the speed of the mixer to medium and incorporate one egg at a time, scraping down the work bowl as needed. Add the vanilla and beat until incorporated.

4 Pour the mixture into the crust, place the cheesecake in a large baking pan with high sides, and gently pour the boiling water into the baking pan until it reaches halfway up the side of the springform pan.

5 Cover the baking pan with aluminum foil, place it in the oven, and bake until the cheesecake is set and only slightly jiggly in the center, 50 minutes to 1 hour.

6 Turn off the oven and leave the oven door cracked. Allow the cheesecake to sit in the cooling oven for 45 minutes.

7 Remove the cheesecake from the oven and transfer it to a cooling rack. Let it sit at room temperature for 1 hour.

8 Transfer the cheesecake to the refrigerator and let it cool for at least 4 hours before serving and slicing.

Classic Cheesecake, see page 197

COOKIES 'N' CREAM CHEESECAKE

YIELD: **1 CHEESECAKE** | ACTIVE TIME: **30 MINUTES** | TOTAL TIME: **8 HOURS**

INGREDIENTS

For the Crust

24 Oreo cookies

6 tablespoons unsalted butter, melted

For the Filling

15 Oreo cookies

2 lbs. cream cheese, softened

⅔ cup sugar

¼ teaspoon kosher salt

4 eggs

1 teaspoon pure vanilla extract

Whipped Cream (see page 248), for serving

1 Preheat the oven to 350°F. To begin preparations for the crust, place the cookies in a food processor and pulse until finely ground. Transfer the crumbs to a medium bowl and combine them with the melted butter.

2 Transfer the mixture to a 9-inch pie plate and press it into the bottom and side in an even layer. Use the bottom of a dry measuring cup to help flatten the bottom of the crust. Use a paring knife to trim away any excess crust and create a flat and smooth edge.

3 Place the pie plate on a baking sheet and bake until it is firm, 8 to 10 minutes. Remove from the oven, transfer the crust to a cooling rack, and let it cool for at least 2 hours.

4 Preheat the oven to 350°F.

5 To begin preparations for the filling, place the cookies in a food processor and pulse until they have the desired texture. Set aside.

6 Bring 8 cups of water to a boil in a small saucepan.

7 In the work bowl of a stand mixer fitted with the paddle attachment, cream the cream cheese, sugar, and salt on high until the mixture is fluffy, about 10 minutes. Scrape down the sides of the work bowl as needed.

8 Reduce the speed of the mixer to medium and incorporate one egg at a time, scraping down the work bowl as needed. Add the vanilla and beat until incorporated. Remove the work bowl from the mixer and fold in the cookie crumbs.

9 Pour the mixture into the crust, place the cheesecake in a large baking pan with high sides, and gently pour the boiling water into the baking pan until it reaches halfway up the sides of the pie plate.

10 Cover the baking pan with aluminum foil, place it in the oven, and bake until the cheesecake is set and only slightly jiggly in the center, 50 minutes to 1 hour.

11 Turn off the oven and leave the oven door cracked. Allow the cheesecake to rest in the cooling oven for 45 minutes.

12 Remove the cheesecake from the oven and transfer it to a cooling rack. Let it sit at room temperature for 1 hour.

13 Refrigerate the cheesecake for at least 4 hours before serving and slicing. To serve, top each slice with a heaping spoonful of Whipped Cream.

BLUEBERRY & LEMON CHEESECAKE

YIELD: **1 CHEESECAKE** | ACTIVE TIME: **1 HOUR** | TOTAL TIME: **8 HOURS**

1 Preheat the oven to 350°F. Bring 8 cups of water to a boil in a medium saucepan.

2 In a small saucepan, cook the blueberries, water, and sugar over medium heat until the blueberries burst and start to become fragrant, about 5 minutes. Remove the pan from heat.

3 In the work bowl of a stand mixer fitted with the paddle attachment, cream the cream cheese, sugar, and salt on high until the mixture is soft and airy, about 10 minutes. Scrape down the side of the work bowl with a rubber spatula as needed.

4 Reduce the speed of the mixer to medium and incorporate the eggs one at a time, scraping down the work bowl as needed. Add the vanilla and mix until incorporated.

5 Divide the mixture between two mixing bowls. Add the blueberry mixture to one bowl and whisk to combine. Whisk the lemon juice into the mixture in the other bowl.

6 Starting with the lemon mixture, add 1 cup to the Graham Cracker Crust. Add 1 cup of the blueberry mixture, and then alternate between the mixtures until all of them have been used.

7 If desired, use a paring knife to gently swirl the blueberry and lemon mixtures together, making sure not to overmix.

8 Place the cheesecake in a large baking pan with high sides. Gently pour the boiling water into the pan until it reaches halfway up the sides of the cheesecake pan. Cover the baking pan with aluminum foil and place it in the oven. Bake until the cheesecake is set and only slightly jiggly in the center, 50 minutes to 1 hour.

9 Turn off the oven and leave the oven door cracked. Allow the cheesecake to sit in the cooling oven for 45 minutes.

10 Remove the cheesecake from the oven and transfer the springform pan to a cooling rack. Let it sit at room temperature for 1 hour.

11 Transfer the cheesecake to the refrigerator and let it cool for at least 4 hours before slicing and serving.

INGREDIENTS

2 pints of blueberries

1 tablespoon water

2 tablespoons sugar

2 lbs. cream cheese, softened

⅔ cup sugar

¼ teaspoon kosher salt

4 eggs

1 teaspoon pure vanilla extract

2 tablespoons fresh lemon juice

1 Graham Cracker Crust (see page 249), in a springform pan

ZEPPOLE

YIELD: **4 SERVINGS** | ACTIVE TIME: **30 MINUTES** | TOTAL TIME: **2 HOURS**

INGREDIENTS

1½ cups all-purpose flour

1 tablespoon plus 1 teaspoon baking powder

¼ teaspoon fine sea salt

2 eggs

2 tablespoons sugar

2 cups ricotta cheese

Zest of 1 orange

1 cup milk

1 teaspoon pure vanilla extract

Canola oil, as needed

¼ cup confectioners' sugar, for dusting

1   Sift the flour, baking powder, and salt into a bowl. Set the mixture aside.

2   Place the eggs and sugar in a separate bowl and whisk to combine. Add the ricotta, whisk to incorporate, and then stir in the orange zest, milk, and vanilla.

3   Gradually incorporate the dry mixture until it comes together as a smooth batter. Place the batter in the refrigerator and chill for 1 hour.

4   Add canola oil to a cast-iron Dutch oven until it is about 2 inches deep and warm it to 350°F. Drop tablespoons of the batter into the hot oil, taking care not to crowd the pot, and fry until the zeppole are golden brown. Transfer the fried zeppole to a paper towel–lined plate and dust them with the confectioners' sugar. Enjoy at room temperature.

RASPBERRY CREAM PIE

YIELD: **1 PIE** | ACTIVE TIME: **15 MINUTES** | TOTAL TIME: **4 HOURS AND 30 MINUTES**

INGREDIENTS

½ lb. cream cheese, softened

1⅔ cups sweetened condensed milk

1½ cups Whipped Cream (see page 248)

1 teaspoon pure vanilla extract

1⅓ cups raspberries

1 Oreo crust (see page 200 for homemade)

1   Place the cream cheese in the work bowl of a stand mixer fitted with the paddle attachment and beat until smooth and creamy.

2   Add the condensed milk and beat the mixture until it is smooth and thick, about 5 minutes. Remove the bowl from the stand mixer, add the Whipped Cream, vanilla, and raspberries, and fold to incorporate.

3   Spoon the filling into the crust and use a rubber spatula to even out the top. Cover with plastic wrap and freeze until set, about 4 hours.

4   To serve, remove the pie from the freezer and let it sit at room temperature for 10 minutes before slicing.

BLUE CHEESE, PEAR & WALNUT GALETTE

YIELD: **1 TART** | ACTIVE TIME: **15 MINUTES** | TOTAL TIME: **1 HOUR**

INGREDIENTS

1 ball of Perfect Piecrust dough (see page 248)

1 pear, cored and sliced thin

1 tablespoon fresh rosemary or thyme

1 cup crumbled blue cheese

1 handful of walnuts

Honey, to taste

1   Preheat the oven to 400°F. Roll the dough out to approximately ¼ inch thick and place it on a parchment-lined baking sheet.

2   Distribute the pear, rosemary, blue cheese, and walnuts evenly over the dough, making sure to leave a 1-inch border at the edge. Fold the uncovered dough over the filling.

3   Place the galette in the oven and bake until the crust is golden brown and the cheese has melted, 35 to 40 minutes.

4   Remove the galette from the oven, let it cool for 5 minutes, and drizzle honey over the top. Slice and enjoy immediately.

Blue Cheese, Pear & Walnut Galette,
see page 207

SQUASH WHOOPIE PIES

YIELD: **12 PIES** | ACTIVE TIME: **20 MINUTES** | TOTAL TIME: **1 HOUR**

1   Preheat the oven to 350°F. Sift the flour, cinnamon, ground ginger, cloves, nutmeg, baking soda, baking powder, and salt into a mixing bowl.

2   Place the brown sugar, maple syrup, pureed squash, egg, and olive oil in a separate mixing bowl and stir until combined. Sift the dry mixture into the squash mixture and stir until it has been incorporated.

3   Use an ice cream scoop to place dollops of the batter onto parchment-lined baking sheets. Make sure to leave plenty of space between the scoops. Place the sheets in the oven and bake until the cakes are golden brown, about 10 to 15 minutes. Remove and let cool.

4   While the squash cakes are cooling, place the remaining ingredients in a bowl and beat with a handheld mixer until the mixture is fluffy.

5   When the cakes have cooled completely, spread the filling on one of the cakes. Top with another cake and repeat until all of the cakes and filling have been used.

INGREDIENTS

1⅓ cups all-purpose flour

1 teaspoon cinnamon

1 teaspoon ground ginger

¼ teaspoon ground cloves

½ teaspoon freshly
grated nutmeg

½ teaspoon baking soda

½ teaspoon baking
powder

1 teaspoon kosher salt

1 cup packed light
brown sugar

2 tablespoons real
maple syrup

1 cup pureed butternut or
acorn squash

1 egg

1 cup extra-virgin olive oil

1⅓ cups confectioners'
sugar

4 tablespoons unsalted
butter

½ lb. cream cheese, at
room temperature

1-inch piece of fresh
ginger, peeled and grated

½ teaspoon pure
vanilla extract

CANNOLI

YIELD: **10 CANNOLI** | ACTIVE TIME: **45 MINUTES** | TOTAL TIME: **4 HOURS**

INGREDIENTS

¾ lb. whole milk
ricotta cheese

¾ lb. mascarpone cheese

4 oz. chocolate, grated

¾ cup confectioners'
sugar, plus more
for dusting

1½ teaspoons pure
vanilla extract

Pinch of fine sea salt

10 cannoli shells

1   Line a colander with three pieces of cheesecloth and place it in the sink. Place the ricotta in the colander, form the cheesecloth into a pouch, and twist to remove as much liquid as possible from the ricotta. Keep the pouch taut and twisted, place it in a baking dish, and place a cast-iron skillet on top. Weigh the skillet down with 2 large, heavy cans and place in the refrigerator for 1 hour.

2   Discard the drained liquid and transfer the ricotta to a mixing bowl. Add the mascarpone, half of the grated chocolate, the confectioners' sugar, vanilla, and salt and stir until well combined. Cover the bowl and refrigerate for at least 1 hour. The mixture will keep in the refrigerator for up to 24 hours.

3   Line an 18 x 13–inch baking sheet with parchment paper. Fill a small saucepan halfway with water and bring it to a gentle simmer. Place the remainder of the chocolate in a heatproof mixing bowl, place it over the simmering water, and stir until it is melted.

4   Dip the ends of the cannoli shells in the chocolate, let the excess drip off, and transfer them to the baking sheet. Let the shells sit until the chocolate is firm, about 1 hour.

5   Place the cannoli filling in a piping bag and cut a ½-inch slit in it. Pipe the filling into the shells, working from both ends in order to ensure they are filled evenly. When all of the cannoli have been filled, dust them with confectioners' sugar and enjoy.

APPLE PIE WITH QUARK

YIELD: **1 PIE** | ACTIVE TIME: **20 MINUTES** | TOTAL TIME: **1 HOUR AND 30 MINUTES**

INGREDIENTS

1 Perfect Piecrust (see page 248), rolled out

½ cup sugar

½ cup unsalted butter, softened

3 large eggs, lightly beaten

2 cups quark cheese

1 teaspoon pure vanilla extract

1 teaspoon lemon zest

1 teaspoon fresh lemon juice

½ cup all-purpose flour

1 teaspoon baking powder

¼ teaspoon kosher salt

3 large Braeburn apples, peeled, cores removed, sliced

⅓ cup slivered almonds

2 tablespoons confectioners' sugar

1   Preheat the oven to 350°F, coat a 9-inch pie plate with nonstick cooking spray, and place the piecrust in it. Place the sugar, butter, eggs, quark, vanilla, lemon zest, and lemon juice in a food processor and puree until smooth, scraping the work bowl as needed.

2   Sift the flour, baking powder, and salt into a mixing bowl. Add the mixture to the food processor and pulse until incorporated. Evenly distribute the mixture in the crust and arrange the apples on top of the mixture.

3   Place the pie in the oven and bake until the filling is set and golden brown, about 40 minutes. Remove from the oven and let cool before serving. To serve, sprinkle the almonds and confectioners' sugar on top.

SNOWBALLS

YIELD: **36 COOKIES** | ACTIVE TIME: **20 MINUTES** | TOTAL TIME: **1 HOUR**

INGREDIENTS

1½ oz. cream cheese, softened

Zest and juice of 1 lime

1½ cups confectioners' sugar

2½ cups all-purpose flour

6 oz. caster sugar

¼ teaspoon fine sea salt

1 cup unsalted butter, softened and divided into tablespoons

2 teaspoons pure vanilla extract

1½ cups sweetened shredded coconut, finely chopped

1   Preheat the oven to 350°F and line two baking sheets with parchment paper. Place 1 tablespoon of the cream cheese and the lime juice in a mixing bowl and stir until the mixture is smooth. Add the confectioners' sugar and whisk until the mixture is smooth and thin, adding lime juice as needed until the glaze reaches the desired consistency. Set aside.

2   Place the flour, caster sugar, salt, and lime zest in a separate mixing bowl and whisk to combine. Add the butter one piece at a time and use a pastry blender to work the mixture until it is a coarse meal. Add the vanilla and remaining cream cheese and work the mixture until it is a smooth dough.

3   Form the mixture into balls and place them on the baking sheets. Place in the oven and bake until the cookies are a light brown, about 15 minutes. Remove from the oven and let cool to room temperature. Brush the glaze over the cookies and sprinkle the coconut on top. Let the glaze set before serving.

MARBLE BROWNIES

YIELD: **16 BROWNIES** | ACTIVE TIME: **15 MINUTES** | TOTAL TIME: **1 HOUR AND 15 MINUTES**

INGREDIENTS

½ cup all-purpose flour, plus more as needed

½ cup unsalted butter

4 oz. milk chocolate chips

3 large eggs, at room temperature

1 cup sugar

Pinch of fine sea salt

½ lb. cream cheese, softened

½ teaspoon pure vanilla extract

1 Preheat the oven to 350°F. Coat a square, 8-inch cake pan with nonstick cooking spray and dust it with flour, knocking out any excess.

2 Fill a small saucepan halfway with water and bring it to a gentle simmer. Place the butter and chocolate chips in a heatproof bowl, place it over the simmering water, and stir until the mixture is melted and smooth. Remove the mixture from heat and let it cool for 5 minutes.

3 Place 2 of the eggs and three-quarters of the sugar in the work bowl of a stand mixer fitted with the paddle attachment and beat on medium speed for 1 minute. Add the chocolate-and-butter mixture, beat for 1 minute, and then add the flour and salt. Beat until just combined and then pour into the prepared pan.

4 In a separate bowl, combine the cream cheese, remaining sugar, remaining egg, and vanilla. Beat with a handheld mixer on medium speed until light and fluffy. Spread on top of the batter and use a fork to stir the layers together. Place in the oven and bake for 35 minutes, until the top is springy to the touch. Remove, allow the brownies to cool in the pan, and then cut into bars.

STRAWBERRY RHUBARB RICOTTA CAKES

YIELD: **4 SMALL CAKES** | ACTIVE TIME: **30 MINUTES** | TOTAL TIME: **1 HOUR AND 15 MINUTES**

INGREDIENTS

For the Cake

½ cup unsalted butter, softened

½ cup sugar

2 eggs

¼ teaspoon pure vanilla extract

Zest of 1 lemon

¾ cup ricotta cheese

¾ cup all-purpose flour

1 teaspoon baking powder

½ teaspoon kosher salt

½ cup minced strawberries, plus more for garnish

½ cup Rhubarb Jam (see page 249)

For the Meringue

1 cup sugar

½ cup water

4 egg whites

1 tablespoon fresh lemon juice

1   Preheat the oven to 350°F and coat a 9 x 5–inch loaf pan with nonstick cooking spray. To begin preparations for the cake, place the butter and sugar in the work bowl of a stand mixer fitted with the paddle attachment and beat on high until the mixture is smooth and a pale yellow. Reduce the speed to medium and incorporate the eggs one at a time, scraping down the work bowl as necessary. Add the vanilla, lemon zest, and ricotta and beat until the mixture is smooth.

2   Place the flour, baking powder, and salt in a mixing bowl and whisk to combine. Reduce the speed of the mixer to low, add the dry mixture to the wet mixture, and beat until it comes together as a smooth batter, scraping down the work bowl as needed.

3   Add the strawberries and fold to incorporate. Place the batter in the loaf pan, place it in the oven, and bake until a cake tester inserted into the center comes out clean, about 35 minutes. Remove the cake from the oven and let it cool to room temperature in the pan.

4   While the cake is in the oven, prepare the meringue. Place the sugar and water in a saucepan and cook on high until the mixture is 240°F. While the simple syrup is heating up, place the egg whites and lemon juice in the mixing bowl of the stand mixer, now fitted with the whisk attachment. Beat at medium speed until soft peaks form, about 2 to 3 minutes. When the simple syrup reaches 240°F, slowly add it to the beaten egg whites with the mixer running. Raise the speed to high and beat until the meringue holds stiff peaks. If desired, transfer the meringue to a pastry bag fitted with a piping tip.

5   Remove the cooled cake from the pan and cut it into 8 pieces. Spread some of the jam over four of the pieces. Cover the jam with some of the meringue and then place the unadorned pieces of cake on top. Spread more meringue on top, garnish with additional strawberries, and serve.

QUARK PANNA COTTA WITH ROSÉ & RASPBERRY SAUCE

YIELD: **6 SERVINGS** | ACTIVE TIME: **40 MINUTES** | TOTAL TIME: **24 HOURS**

INGREDIENTS

For the Panna Cotta

2½ cups heavy cream

⅔ cup whole milk

⅔ cup sugar

½ teaspoon fine sea salt

1 teaspoon pure
vanilla extract

2 cups quark cheese

½ oz. gelatin (2 envelopes)

6 tablespoons honey

Raspberries, for garnish

Toasted almonds,
for garnish

Fresh mint leaves,
for garnish

For the Sauce

2 cups Rosé

⅓ cup sugar

¼ teaspoon fine sea salt

2 cups raspberries

1   To prepare the panna cotta, place the cream, milk, sugar, salt, and vanilla in a saucepan and bring to a simmer over medium heat, taking care that the mixture does not come to a boil. Remove the pan from heat.

2   Place the quark in a small mixing bowl and ladle about 1 cup of the warm milk mixture into the bowl. Whisk to combine and then pour the tempered quark into the saucepan.

3   Bring the mixture back to a simmer and then remove the saucepan from heat. Place the gelatin in a large mixing bowl and pour the warmed mixture into it, whisking constantly to prevent lumps from forming. Pour the mixture into six ramekins and place them in the refrigerator to set overnight.

4   Approximately 2 hours before you will serve the panna cotta, prepare the sauce. Place the Rosé in a small saucepan and cook over medium-high heat until it has reduced by half. Add the remaining ingredients for the sauce, bring the mixture to a boil, and then reduce the heat so that the mixture simmers. Simmer for 20 minutes.

5   Transfer the mixture to a blender and puree until smooth. Strain through a fine sieve and place the sauce in the refrigerator to cool completely.

6   When the panna cottas are set, pour 1 tablespoon of honey over each serving. Pour the sauce on top of the honey and garnish with raspberries, toasted almonds, and mint.

TIRAMISU

YIELD: **8 TO 10 SERVINGS** | ACTIVE TIME: **20 MINUTES** | TOTAL TIME: **3 HOURS AND 30 MINUTES**

INGREDIENTS

2 cups freshly brewed espresso

½ cup plus 1 tablespoon sugar

3 tablespoons Kahlúa

4 large egg yolks

2 cups mascarpone cheese

1 cup heavy cream

30 Ladyfingers (see page 250)

2 tablespoons unsweetened cocoa powder

1   Place the espresso, 1 tablespoon of the sugar, and the Kahlúa in a bowl and stir to combine. Set the mixture aside.

2   Place two inches of water in a saucepan and bring to a simmer. Place the remaining sugar and egg yolks in a metal mixing bowl and set the bowl over the simmering water. Whisk the mixture continually until it has nearly tripled in size, approximately 10 minutes. Remove from heat, add the mascarpone, and fold to incorporate.

3   Pour the heavy cream into a separate bowl and whisk until soft peaks start to form. Gently fold the whipped cream into the mascarpone mixture.

4   Place the Ladyfingers in the espresso mixture and briefly submerge them. Place an even layer of the soaked Ladyfingers on the bottom of a 9 x 13–inch baking pan. This will use up approximately half of the Ladyfingers. Spread half of the mascarpone mixture on top of the Ladyfingers and then repeat until the Ladyfingers and mascarpone have been used up.

5   Cover with plastic and place in the refrigerator for 3 hours. Sprinkle the cocoa powder over the top before serving.

BAKED APPLES

YIELD: **6 SERVINGS** | ACTIVE TIME: **15 MINUTES** | TOTAL TIME: **1 HOUR**

INGREDIENTS

6 apples

3 tablespoons unsalted butter, melted

6 tablespoons blackberry jam

2 oz. goat cheese, softened, cut into 6 rounds

1 Preheat the oven to 350°F. Slice the tops off of the apples and set them aside. Use a paring knife to cut out the apples' cores and then scoop out the centers, leaving a ½-inch-thick wall inside each apple.

2 Rub the inside and outside of the apples with some of the melted butter. Place the jam and goat cheese in a mixing bowl and stir to combine. Fill the apples' cavities with the mixture, place the tops back on the apples, and set them aside.

3 Coat a baking pan with the remaining butter and then arrange the apples in the pan. Place in the oven and bake until tender, 25 to 30 minutes. Remove from the oven and let cool briefly before serving.

BEET PANNA COTTA

YIELD: **4 SERVINGS** | ACTIVE TIME: **30 MINUTES** | TOTAL TIME: **4 HOURS AND 30 MINUTES**

INGREDIENTS

4 sheets of silver gelatin

13 oz. heavy cream

9 oz. milk

4 oz. sugar

1¾ oz. honey

¾ lb. red beets, peeled and finely diced

4 oz. goat cheese, crumbled

1   Place the gelatin sheets in a small bowl. Add 1 cup of ice and water until the sheets are submerged. Let the mixture rest.

2   Combine the heavy cream, milk, sugar, honey, and beets in a saucepan and bring to a simmer. Cook for 15 minutes and then remove the pan from heat.

3   Remove the bloomed gelatin from the ice water. Squeeze to remove as much water from the sheets as possible, add them to the warm mixture, and whisk until they have completely dissolved.

4   Transfer the mixture to a blender, add the goat cheese, and puree until emulsified, about 45 seconds.

5   Strain the mixture into a bowl through a fine-mesh sieve and divide it among four 8-oz. ramekins, leaving about ½ inch of space at the top. Carefully transfer the ramekins to the refrigerator and chill until the panna cottas are fully set, about 4 hours.

THE PERFECT FLAN

YIELD: **6 SERVINGS** | ACTIVE TIME: **30 MINUTES** | TOTAL TIME: **6 HOURS AND 30 MINUTES**

INGREDIENTS

2 cups sugar

¼ cup water

5 egg yolks

5 eggs

5 oz. cream cheese, softened

1 (14 oz.) can of sweetened condensed milk

1 (12 oz.) can of evaporated milk

1½ cups heavy cream

½ teaspoon almond extract

½ teaspoon pure vanilla extract

1   Preheat the oven to 350°F. Bring 2 quarts of water to a boil and set aside.

2   Place 1 cup of the sugar and the water in a small saucepan and bring to a boil over high heat, swirling the pan instead of stirring. Cook until the caramel is a deep golden brown, taking care not to burn it. Remove the pan from heat and pour the caramel into a round 8-inch cake pan. Place the cake pan on a cooling rack and let it sit until it has set.

3   Place the egg yolks, eggs, cream cheese, remaining sugar, condensed milk, evaporated milk, heavy cream, almond extract, and vanilla in a blender and puree until emulsified.

4   Pour the mixture over the caramel and place the cake pan in a roasting pan. Pour the boiling water into the roasting pan until it reaches halfway up the side of the cake pan.

5   Place the flan in the oven and bake until it is just set, 60 to 70 minutes. The flan should still be jiggly without being runny. Remove from the oven, place the cake pan on a cooling rack, and let it cool for 1 hour.

6   Place the flan in the refrigerator and chill for 4 hours.

7   Run a knife along the edge of the pan and invert the flan onto a plate so that the caramel layer is on top. Slice the flan and serve.

LEMON TARTS

YIELD: **24 TARTS** | ACTIVE TIME: **20 MINUTES** | TOTAL TIME: **1 HOUR**

INGREDIENTS

For the Dough

¾ cup unsalted butter, softened

3 oz. cream cheese, softened

1½ cups all-purpose flour

½ cup confectioners' sugar

For the Filling

2 cups sugar

5 tablespoons all-purpose flour

4 eggs

Zest and juice of 2 lemons

Confectioners' sugar, for dusting

1   To prepare the dough, place the butter and cream cheese in the work bowl of a stand mixer and beat until just combined. Place the flour and confectioners' sugar in a separate bowl and whisk to combine. Add the dry mixture to the butter-and-cream cheese mixture and beat until it just comes together as a dough. Work the mixture with your hands until it is smooth and homogenous.

2   Spoon approximately 1 tablespoon of dough into the wells of an ungreased miniature tart pan. Using your fingers, press down on the dough so that it fills the wells. Set the pan aside and preheat the oven to 350°F.

3   To prepare the filling, combine the sugar and flour in the work bowl of a stand mixer fitted with the whisk attachment. Add the eggs and beat until incorporated, scraping down the work bowl as needed. Add the lemon zest and juice and beat until incorporated.

4   Fill the tart shells with the filling, place the tarts in the oven, and bake until the shells are golden brown, about 20 minutes. Remove and let cool in the pan for 15 minutes.

5   Run a knife around the edge of each tart, remove them from the pan, dust them with confectioners' sugar, and enjoy.

TIP: Add blueberries or raspberries to the lemon filling for a delicious, fruit-filled variation!

APPENDIX

PICKLED RAMPS

YIELD: **2 SERVINGS** | ACTIVE TIME: **5 MINUTES** | TOTAL TIME: **2 HOURS**

INGREDIENTS

½ cup champagne vinegar

½ cup water

¼ cup sugar

1½ teaspoons kosher salt

¼ teaspoon fennel seeds

¼ teaspoon coriander seeds

⅛ teaspoon red pepper flakes

10 small ramps

1   Place all of the ingredients, except for the ramps, in a small saucepan and bring to a boil over medium heat.

2   Add the ramps, reduce the heat, and simmer for 1 minute.

3   Transfer the ramps and the brine to a mason jar, cover with plastic wrap, and let cool completely. Once cool, cover with a lid and store in the refrigerator for up to 1 month.

AIOLI

YIELD: **1 CUP** | ACTIVE TIME: **5 MINUTES** | TOTAL TIME: **5 MINUTES**

INGREDIENTS

2 large egg yolks

2 teaspoons Dijon mustard

2 teaspoons fresh lemon juice

1 garlic clove, mashed

¾ cup canola oil

¼ cup extra-virgin olive oil

Salt and pepper, to taste

1   Place the egg yolks, mustard, lemon juice, and garlic in a food processor and blitz until combined.

2   With the food processor running on low, slowly drizzle in the oils until they are emulsified. If the aioli becomes too thick for your liking, stir in water 1 teaspoon at a time until it has thinned out.

3   Season the aioli with salt and pepper and use as desired.

SAVORY TART SHELLS

YIELD: **2 TART SHELLS** | ACTIVE TIME: **30 MINUTES** | TOTAL TIME: **2 HOURS**

INGREDIENTS

2½ cups all-purpose flour, plus more as needed

⅓ cup extra-virgin olive oil

½ cup ice water

1 teaspoon fine sea salt

1 Place all of the ingredients in a bowl and work the mixture until it comes together as a dough. Divide the dough into two pieces, flatten them into disks, wrap them in plastic, and refrigerate for 1 hour.

2 Preheat the oven to 400°F. Coat two 9-inch pie plates with nonstick cooking spray. Place the pieces of dough on a flour-dusted work surface and roll them out into ¼-inch-thick rounds. Lay the crusts in the pie plates, trim away any excess, and prick the bottom of the crusts with a fork. Cover the crusts with aluminum foil, fill the foil with uncooked rice, dried beans, or pie weights, and place them in the oven. Bake the crusts until they are firm and golden brown, about 20 minutes.

3 Remove the tart shells from the oven, remove the foil and weights, and fill the tart shells as desired.

Note: If not using right away, store in the refrigerator for up to 1 week or in the freezer for up to 6 months.

ZUCCHINI CREAM

YIELD: **½ CUP** | ACTIVE TIME: **20 MINUTES** | TOTAL TIME: **20 MINUTES**

INGREDIENTS

2 tablespoons extra-virgin olive oil

1 zucchini, chopped

½ onion, chopped

Salt and pepper, to taste

1 Coat the bottom of a large skillet with half of the olive oil and warm it over medium heat. Add the zucchini and onion and cook, stirring occasionally, until they are tender, about 10 minutes.

2 Season the vegetables with salt and pepper, raise the heat to medium-high, and cook until all of the liquid in the pan has evaporated.

3 Place the sautéed vegetables in a blender or food processor, add the remaining olive oil, and puree until smooth.

236 | THE DELICIOUSLY CHEESY COOKBOOK

PICADILLO DE RES

YIELD: **4 SERVINGS** | ACTIVE TIME: **10 MINUTES** | TOTAL TIME: **35 MINUTES**

INGREDIENTS

2 tablespoons extra-virgin olive oil

2 lbs. ground beef

Salt, to taste

1 teaspoon cumin

1½ teaspoons dried Mexican oregano

1½ teaspoons chili powder

1 tablespoon tomato paste

1 onion, finely diced

2 serrano chile peppers, stems and seeds removed, chopped

2 bay leaves

1 lb. Yukon Gold potatoes, peeled and diced

½ lb. carrots, peeled and finely diced

3 large tomatoes, finely diced

½ cup peas (optional)

1 Place the olive oil in a large skillet and warm it over medium heat. Add the ground beef, season it with salt, and cook, breaking the meat up with a wooden spoon, until browned, about 6 minutes.

2 Stir in the cumin, oregano, and chili powder, cook for 1 minute, and then stir in the tomato paste, onion, and peppers. Cook, stirring occasionally, until the onion is tender, about 5 minutes.

3 Add the bay leaves, potatoes, carrots, and tomatoes and cook until the potatoes are tender and the flavors have developed to your liking, about 20 minutes. If using peas in the dish, add them during the last 5 minutes of cooking the potatoes.

4 Use as a filling for the Chiles en Nogada on page 113, empanadas, or tacos, or enjoy on its own.

BEEF STOCK

YIELD: **8 CUPS** | ACTIVE TIME: **20 MINUTES** | TOTAL TIME: **6 HOURS**

INGREDIENTS

7 lbs. beef bones, rinsed

4 cups chopped yellow onions

2 cups chopped carrots

2 cups chopped celery

3 garlic cloves, crushed

3 sprigs of fresh thyme

1 teaspoon black peppercorns

1 bay leaf

1 Place the beef bones in a stockpot and cover them with cold water. Bring to a simmer over medium-high heat and use a ladle to skim off any impurities that rise to the surface.

2 Add the vegetables, thyme, peppercorns, and bay leaf, reduce the heat to low, and simmer for 5 hours, occasionally skimming the stock to remove any impurities that rise to the surface.

3 Strain the stock, let it cool slightly, and transfer it to the refrigerator. Leave the stock uncovered and let it cool completely. Remove the layer of fat and cover. The stock will keep in the refrigerator for 3 to 5 days, and in the freezer for up to 3 months.

CHICKEN STOCK

YIELD: **8 CUPS** | ACTIVE TIME: **20 MINUTES** | TOTAL TIME: **6 HOURS**

INGREDIENTS

7 lbs. chicken bones, rinsed

4 cups chopped yellow onions

2 cups chopped carrots

2 cups chopped celery

3 garlic cloves, crushed

3 sprigs of fresh thyme

1 teaspoon black peppercorns

1 bay leaf

1   Place the chicken bones in a stockpot and cover them with cold water. Bring to a simmer over medium-high heat and use a ladle to skim off any impurities that rise to the surface.

2   Add the vegetables, thyme, peppercorns, and bay leaf, reduce the heat to low, and simmer for 5 hours, skimming the stock occasionally to remove any impurities that rise to the surface.

3   Strain the stock, let it cool slightly, and transfer it to the refrigerator. Leave the stock uncovered and let it cool completely. Remove the layer of fat and cover. The stock will keep in the refrigerator for 3 to 5 days, and in the freezer for up to 3 months.

VEGETABLE STOCK

YIELD: **6 CUPS** | ACTIVE TIME: **20 MINUTES** | TOTAL TIME: **3 HOURS**

INGREDIENTS

2 tablespoons extra-virgin olive oil

2 large leeks, trimmed and rinsed well

2 large carrots, peeled and sliced

2 celery stalks, sliced

2 large yellow onions, sliced

3 garlic cloves, unpeeled but smashed

2 sprigs of fresh parsley

2 sprigs of fresh thyme

1 bay leaf

8 cups water

½ teaspoon black peppercorns

Salt, to taste

1   Place the olive oil and the vegetables in a large stockpot and cook over low heat until the liquid they release has evaporated. This will allow the flavor of the vegetables to become concentrated.

2   Add the garlic, parsley, thyme, bay leaf, water, peppercorns, and salt. Raise the heat to high and bring to a boil. Reduce the heat so that the stock simmers and cook for 2 hours, while skimming to remove any impurities that float to the surface.

3   Strain through a fine sieve, let the stock cool slightly, and place in the refrigerator, uncovered, to chill. Remove the fat layer and cover the stock. The stock will keep in the refrigerator for 3 to 5 days, and in the freezer for up to 3 months.

BALSAMIC GLAZE

YIELD: ½ CUP | ACTIVE TIME: **10 MINUTES** | TOTAL TIME: **25 MINUTES**

INGREDIENTS

1 cup balsamic vinegar

¼ cup brown sugar

1 Place the vinegar and sugar in a small saucepan and bring the mixture to a boil.

2 Reduce the heat to medium-low and simmer for 8 to 10 minutes, stirring frequently, until the mixture has thickened.

3 Remove the pan from heat and let the glaze cool for 15 minutes before using.

EVERYTHING SEASONING

YIELD: ½ CUP | ACTIVE TIME: **5 MINUTES** | TOTAL TIME: **5 MINUTES**

INGREDIENTS

2 tablespoons poppy seeds

1 tablespoon fennel seeds

1 tablespoon onion flakes

1 tablespoon garlic flakes

2 tablespoons sesame seeds

1 Place all of the ingredients in a mixing bowl and stir to combine. Use immediately or store in an airtight container until ready to use.

CILANTRO PESTO

YIELD: **1½ CUPS** | ACTIVE TIME: **5 MINUTES** | TOTAL TIME: **5 MINUTES**

INGREDIENTS

1 cup fresh cilantro

1 garlic clove, chopped

¼ cup sunflower seeds

¼ cup shredded queso enchilado

¼ cup extra-virgin olive oil

1 teaspoon fresh lemon juice

Salt and pepper, to taste

1 Place all of the ingredients in a food processor and blitz until the mixture has emulsified. Use immediately or store in the refrigerator.

PICO DE GALLO

YIELD: **1 CUP** | ACTIVE TIME: **10 MINUTES** | TOTAL TIME: **1 HOUR AND 10 MINUTES**

INGREDIENTS

4 plum tomatoes, diced

1 jalapeño chile pepper, stem and seeds removed, chopped

½ cup chopped red onion

¼ cup chopped fresh cilantro

Zest and juice of ½ lime

Salt, to taste

1 Place the tomatoes, jalapeño, red onion, cilantro, lime zest, and lime juice in a mixing bowl and stir to combine.

2 Season the salsa with salt and refrigerate it for 1 hour before serving.

CORN TORTILLAS

YIELD: **32 TORTILLAS** | ACTIVE TIME: **30 MINUTES** | TOTAL TIME: **30 MINUTES**

INGREDIENTS

1 lb. masa harina

1½ tablespoons kosher salt

3 cups warm filtered water, plus more as needed

1   In the work bowl of stand mixer fitted with the paddle attachment, combine the masa harina and salt. With the mixer on low speed, slowly begin to add the water. The mixture should come together as a soft, smooth dough. You want the masa to be moist enough so that when a small ball of it is pressed flat in your hands the edges do not crack. Also, the masa should not stick to your hands when you peel it off your palm.

2   Let the masa rest for 10 minutes and check the hydration again. You may need to add more water, depending on environmental conditions.

3   Warm a cast-iron skillet over high heat. Portion the masa into 1-ounce balls and cover them with a damp linen towel.

4   Line a tortilla press with two 8-inch circles of plastic. You can use a grocery store bag, a resealable bag, or even a standard kitchen trash bag as a source for the plastic. Place a ball of masa in the center of one circle and gently push down on it with the palm of one hand to flatten it. Place the other plastic circle on top and then close the tortilla press, applying firm, even pressure to flatten the masa into a round tortilla.

5   Open the tortilla press and remove the top layer of plastic. Carefully pick up the tortilla and remove the bottom piece of plastic.

6   Gently lay the tortilla flat in the pan, taking care to not wrinkle it. Cook for 15 to 30 seconds, until the edges begin to lift up slightly. Turn the tortilla over and let it cook for 30 to 45 seconds before turning it over one last time. If the hydration of the masa was correct and the heat is high enough, the tortilla should puff up and inflate. Remove the tortilla from the pan and store in a tortilla warmer lined with a linen towel. Repeat until all of the prepared masa has been made into tortillas.

WONTON WRAPPERS

YIELD: **48 WRAPPERS** | ACTIVE TIME: **1 HOUR** | TOTAL TIME: **3 HOURS**

INGREDIENTS

¼ cup water, plus more
as needed

1 large egg

¾ teaspoon kosher salt

1½ cups all-purpose flour,
plus more as needed

Cornstarch, as needed

1   Place the water, egg, and salt in a measuring cup and whisk to combine. Place the flour in the work bowl of a stand mixer fitted with the paddle attachment. With the mixer running on low speed, add the egg mixture in a steady stream and beat until the mixture just comes together, adding water or flour in ½-teaspoon increments if the dough is too dry or too wet, respectively.

2   Fit the mixer with the dough hook and knead the dough at medium speed until it is soft, smooth, and springs back quickly when poked with a finger, about 10 minutes. Cover the bowl tightly with plastic wrap and let it rest for 2 hours.

3   Cut the dough into three pieces. Working with one piece at a time (cover the others tightly with plastic wrap), shape the dough into a ball. Place the dough on a flour-dusted work surface and roll it out into a rectangle that is about ½ inch thick. Feed the dough through a pasta maker, adjusting the setting to reduce the thickness with each pass, until the dough is a thin sheet, thin enough that you can see your hand through it (about 1⁄16 inch thick). Place the sheets on a parchment-lined baking sheet.

4   Dust a work surface with cornstarch and cut the sheets into as many 4-inch squares or 3-inch rounds as possible. Pile the cut wrappers on top of each other and fill as desired or cover in plastic wrap and store in the refrigerator for up to 3 days.

MARINARA SAUCE

YIELD: **8 CUPS** | ACTIVE TIME: **20 MINUTES** | TOTAL TIME: **2 HOURS**

INGREDIENTS

4 lbs. tomatoes, quartered

1 large yellow onion, sliced

15 garlic cloves, crushed

2 teaspoons finely chopped fresh thyme

2 teaspoons finely chopped fresh oregano

2 tablespoons extra-virgin olive oil

1½ tablespoons kosher salt

1 teaspoon black pepper

2 tablespoons finely chopped fresh basil

1 tablespoon finely chopped fresh parsley

1 Place all of the ingredients, except for the basil and parsley, in a Dutch oven and cook over medium heat, stirring constantly, until the tomatoes release their liquid and begin to collapse, about 10 minutes.

2 Reduce the heat to low and cook, stirring occasionally, for about 1½ hours, or until the flavor is to your liking.

3 Stir in the basil and parsley and season to taste. The sauce will be chunky. If you prefer a smoother texture, transfer the sauce to a blender and puree before serving.

SALSA VERDE

YIELD: **1½ CUPS** | ACTIVE TIME: **20 MINUTES** | TOTAL TIME: **20 MINUTES**

INGREDIENTS

1 lb. tomatillos, husked and rinsed

5 garlic cloves, unpeeled

1 small white onion, quartered

10 serrano chile peppers

2 bunches of fresh cilantro

Salt, to taste

1 Warm a cast-iron skillet over high heat. Place the tomatillos, garlic, onion, and chiles in the pan and cook until charred all over, turning them occasionally.

2 Remove the vegetables from the pan and let them cool slightly.

3 Peel the garlic cloves and remove the stems and seeds from the chiles. Place the charred vegetables in a blender, add the cilantro, and puree until smooth.

4 Season the salsa with salt and enjoy.

GUACAMOLE

YIELD: **4 SERVINGS** | ACTIVE TIME: **15 MINUTES** | TOTAL TIME: **25 MINUTES**

INGREDIENTS

1 large tomato, finely diced

2 serrano chile peppers, stems and seeds removed, finely diced

½ onion, finely diced

1 garlic clove, mashed

4 large avocados, pitted and diced

6 tablespoons fresh lime juice

Salt, to taste

½ cup fresh cilantro, chopped

1 Combine the tomato, chiles, and onion in a bowl. Place the garlic clove in a separate bowl.

2 Add the avocados to the bowl containing the garlic and stir until well combined. Stir in the lime juice and season with salt.

3 Add the tomato mixture and stir until it has been incorporated. Add the cilantro and stir to combine. Taste and adjust the seasoning as necessary.

FLOUR TORTILLAS

YIELD: **18 TORTILLAS** | ACTIVE TIME: **45 MINUTES** | TOTAL TIME: **1 HOUR AND 30 MINUTES**

INGREDIENTS

1 lb. all-purpose flour, plus more as needed

1 tablespoon kosher salt

1 tablespoon baking powder

2½ oz. lard or unsalted butter, melted

8 to 10 oz. warm, filtered water (105°F)

1   In the work bowl of a stand mixer fitted with the paddle attachment, combine the flour, salt, and baking powder and beat on low speed for 30 seconds.

2   Gradually add the lard and beat until the mixture is a coarse meal.

3   Fit the mixer with the dough hook and set it to low speed. Add the water in a slow stream until the dough begins to come together, 2 to 3 minutes. The dough should begin to pull away from the sides of the mixing bowl, leaving no residue behind. Increase the speed to medium and continue mixing until the dough becomes very soft, shiny, and elastic. Please note that more or less of the water may be required due to environmental conditions and/or variations in the flour.

4   Remove the dough from the work bowl and place it in a mixing bowl. Cover with plastic wrap or a damp kitchen towel and let it rest at room temperature for 30 to 45 minutes.

5   Portion the dough into rounds the size of golf balls, approximately 1½ oz. each. Using the palms of your hands, roll the rounds in a circular motion until they are seamless balls. Place on a parchment-lined baking sheet and cover with plastic wrap. Let them rest at room temperature for 20 minutes.

6   Working on a very smooth and flour-dusted work surface, roll out the balls of dough until they are between ⅛ and ¼ inch thick and about 8 inches in diameter. Stack the tortillas, separating each one with pieces of parchment paper that have been cut to size.

7   Warm a cast-iron skillet over medium-high heat. Gently place a tortilla in the pan. It should immediately sizzle and start to puff up. Do not puncture it. Cook, turning frequently, for 20 to 30 seconds per side, until lightly golden brown in spots. Stack in a linen towel, tortilla warmer, or plastic resealable bag so it continues to steam and repeat with the remaining tortillas.

PERFECT PIECRUSTS

YIELD: 2 (9-INCH) PIECRUSTS | ACTIVE TIME: 15 MINUTES | TOTAL TIME: 2 HOURS AND 15 MINUTES

INGREDIENTS

1 cup unsalted butter, cubed

2½ cups all-purpose flour, plus more as needed

½ teaspoon kosher salt

4 teaspoons sugar

½ cup ice water

1 Transfer the butter to a small bowl and place it in the freezer.

2 Place the flour, salt, and sugar in a food processor and pulse a few times until combined.

3 Add the chilled butter and pulse until the mixture is crumbly, consisting of pea-sized clumps.

4 Add the water and pulse until the mixture comes together as a dough.

5 Place the dough on a flour-dusted work surface and fold it over itself until it is a ball. Divide the dough in two and flatten each piece into a 1-inch-thick disk. Cover each piece completely with plastic wrap and place the dough in the refrigerator for at least 2 hours before rolling it out to fit your pie plate.

WHIPPED CREAM

YIELD: 2 CUPS | ACTIVE TIME: 5 MINUTES | TOTAL TIME: 5 MINUTES

INGREDIENTS

2 cups heavy cream

3 tablespoons sugar

1 teaspoon pure vanilla extract

1 In the work bowl of a stand mixer fitted with the whisk attachment, whip the heavy cream, sugar, and vanilla on high until the mixture holds soft peaks.

2 Use immediately, or store in the refrigerator for up to 3 days.

GRAHAM CRACKER CRUST

YIELD: **1 (9-INCH) CRUST** | ACTIVE TIME: **10 MINUTES** | TOTAL TIME: **1 HOUR**

INGREDIENTS

1½ cups graham cracker crumbs

2 tablespoons sugar

1 tablespoon pure maple syrup

6 tablespoons unsalted butter, melted

1 Preheat the oven to 375°F. Place the graham cracker crumbs and sugar in a large mixing bowl and stir to combine. Add the maple syrup and 5 tablespoons of the melted butter and stir until thoroughly combined.

2 Coat a 9-inch cast-iron skillet with the remaining butter. Pour the graham cracker mixture into the pan and gently press it into shape. Line the crust with aluminum paper, fill it with uncooked rice, dried beans, or pie weights, and place the pan in the oven. Bake for about 10 minutes, until the crust is firm.

3 Remove the pan from the oven, discard the aluminum foil and weights, and allow the crust to cool completely before filling.

RHUBARB JAM

YIELD: **4 CUPS** | ACTIVE TIME: **25 MINUTES** | TOTAL TIME: **4 HOURS**

INGREDIENTS

4 cups chopped rhubarb

1 cup water

¾ cup sugar

½ teaspoon kosher salt

1 teaspoon pectin

1 Place the rhubarb, water, sugar, and salt in a saucepan and cook the mixture over high heat, stirring occasionally, until nearly all of the liquid has evaporated.

2 Add the pectin and stir the mixture for 1 minute.

3 Transfer the jam to a sterilized mason jar and let it cool completely before applying the lid and placing the jam in the refrigerator, where it will keep for up to 1 week.

LADYFINGERS

YIELD: **30 LADYFINGERS** | ACTIVE TIME: **15 MINUTES** | TOTAL TIME: **1 HOUR**

INGREDIENTS

⅔ cup all-purpose flour, plus more as needed

3 eggs, separated

½ cup plus 1 tablespoon sugar

1 teaspoon pure vanilla extract

Pinch of fine sea salt

¾ cup confectioners' sugar

1   Preheat the oven to 300°F. Line two baking sheets with parchment paper and dust them with flour.

2   Place the egg yolks in a mixing bowl and gradually incorporate the sugar, using a handheld mixer at high speed. When the mixture is thick and a pale yellow, whisk in the vanilla.

3   In the work bowl of a stand mixer fitted with the whisk attachment, beat the egg whites and salt until the mixture holds soft peaks. Scoop one-quarter of the whipped egg whites into the egg yolk mixture and sift one-quarter of the flour on top. Fold to combine and repeat until all of the egg whites and flour have been incorporated and the mixture is light and airy.

4   Spread the batter in 4-inch-long strips on the baking sheets, leaving 1 inch between them. Sprinkle the confectioners' sugar over the top of each cookie and place them in the oven.

5   Bake the ladyfingers until they are lightly golden brown and just crispy, about 20 minutes. Remove from the oven and transfer the ladyfingers to a wire rack to cool completely before using.

METRIC CONVERSIONS

U.S. Measurement	Approximate Metric Liquid Measurement	Approximate Metric Dry Measurement
1 teaspoon	5 ml	5 g
1 tablespoon or ½ ounce	15 ml	14 g
1 ounce or ⅛ cup	30 ml	29 g
¼ cup or 2 ounces	60 ml	57 g
⅓ cup	80 ml	76 g
½ cup or 4 ounces	120 ml	113 g
⅔ cup	160 ml	151 g
¾ cup or 6 ounces	180 ml	170 g
1 cup or 8 ounces or ½ pint	240 ml	227 g
1½ cups or 12 ounces	350 ml	340 g
2 cups or 1 pint or 16 ounces	475 ml	454 g
3 cups or 1½ pints	700 ml	680 g
4 cups or 2 pints or 1 quart	950 ml	908 g

INDEX

ABOUT CIDER MILL PRESS BOOK PUBLISHERS

Good ideas ripen with time. From seed to harvest, Cider Mill Press brings fine reading, information, and entertainment together between the covers of its creatively crafted books. Our Cider Mill bears fruit twice a year, publishing a new crop of titles each spring and fall.

"Where Good Books Are Ready for Press"

501 Nelson Place
Nashville, Tennessee 37214

cidermillpress.com